BASIC HISTORY OF THE CONFEDERACY

FRANK E. VANDIVER

*Chairman of the Department of History
at Rice University*

AN ANVIL ORIGINAL
under the general editorship of
LOUIS L. SNYDER

D. VAN NOSTRAND COMPANY, INC.
PRINCETON, NEW JERSEY
TORONTO   LONDON
NEW YORK

For
ALAN and MARJORIE CHAPMAN

D. VAN NOSTRAND COMPANY, INC.
120 Alexander St., Princeton, New Jersey (*Principal office*); 24 West 40 St., New York, N.Y.
D. VAN NOSTRAND COMPANY (Canada), LTD.
25 Hollinger Rd., Toronto 16, Canada
D. VAN NOSTRAND COMPANY, LTD.
358, Kensington High Street, London, W.14, England

PRINTED IN THE UNITED STATES OF AMERICA

PREFACE

The Confederacy lived briefly but violently, and because it was born in conflict and sustained by sacrifice, the years of its history loom larger than most. Above all Confederates wanted independence. Beyond that they wanted to preserve the "Southern way of life," a dream dimly understood and poorly articulated, but which certainly included slaves, cotton, abundant land, planters, and a graciousness of living fashioned in Cavalier romances. Confederates fought for what they thought was right and virtuous. It happened that they set their faces against the tide of history and strove mightily to achieve a nationalism different from the rest of the Western World. It also, and perhaps consequently, happened that they failed. But they failed in a way to earn them a lasting place in American history—a place deserving of far more space than this small volume. What is attempted here is a bare outline of their life and desperate times.

My special thanks, as always, to my wife Susie, who pored over these pages with a critical eye. And many thanks, too, to Mr. Thomas Lawrence Connelly, a long-suffering graduate assistant, who did yeomen service in checking references and compiling statistics.

Rice University FRANK E. VANDIVER
May, 1961

3

TABLE OF CONTENTS

Part 1

A BASIC HISTORY OF THE CONFEDERACY

— 1 —

"WE, THE PEOPLE OF THE CONFEDERATE STATES . . ."

Secession of Southern States. Lincoln's election to the Presidency was the spark which ignited South Carolina. When the results of the election were known, a convention of the people assembled and took the Palmetto State out of the Union on December 20, 1860. The Ordinance of Secession of South Carolina, based on the compact theory of the federal system, announced that the state once more had taken its place among the sovereign nations of the earth. (*See Document No. 1.*)

For years, ever since the tariff crisis of 1832, South Carolina and other Southern states had threatened nullification and secession. Threats had grown old and lost their impact, so when secession came it was something of a surprise to the North. Some Southerners were surprised, too, for many were used to political bombast and boasting as a means of maintaining the Southern position in the national Congress. Disunion had been talked and planned, but over these caucuses and plots lurked an aura of histrionics. Words were one thing; deeds another. Now South Carolina cast the die. The South had to face the issue of helping a sister state or staying in a Union marching steadily on the road to centralization and abolition.

South Carolina leaders knew from past experience the powers of inertia that kept the Cotton South talking instead of acting. Some of them felt the only way to overcome this inertia was to take the plunge. South Carolina took it and asked that she not be left to stand alone. To minimize risk, Palmetto State representatives were sent to the legislatures of sister states as heralds of independence and to urge a new combination of Deep South republics in another confederacy.

Secession generated its own enthusiasm. Fear of a Black Republican president and of the economic and social policies of his party lent power to secessionists everywhere. Conventions were called across the South; secession ordinances drafted. Mississippi seceded on January 9, followed by Florida the next day, and by Alabama on the 11th. Georgia withdrew on January 19; Louisiana exactly a week later. Texas submitted the issue of secession to the people and left the Union on February 1.

Southern "Tories." Excitement had much to do with spurring secession. Union sentiment remained strong in the South, and might have curbed radicalism had not a crescendo of Southern nationalism overwhelmed most of the moderates. It became impossible, as it always does, to be mild or neutral—those not with secession were against it. Secession itself finished the fence-sitters, and many who doubted the wisdom of disunion cast their lot with their native states. Numerous Unionists of the South shared the idea that sovereignty lay with the states, that a man's loyalty should be given to the closest government, and that the United States had second claim on patriotism. A few in the South who remained loyal to the United States were the "Tories" of the Confederacy; they suffered as did their earlier counterparts. In general, though, a spirit of Southern unity prevailed.

Formation of Confederate Government. Southern political leaders knew too well the plight of the nation under the Articles of Confederation to believe that the various states could exist without some form of federal organization—especially should the Union decide to resist secession. The creation of a new government became an urgent necessity, and delegates of the first six Southern republics met at Montgomery, Alabama, on February 4, 1861, to plan an organization. Texas sent a delegation, but too late to take part in constructing a provisional government for the South.

Moderation prevailed at the Montgomery Convention. Although the South actually launched a revolution, few of the real revolutionary, fire-eater leaders were elected to the Convention, and those who were had small voice in its activities. Howel Cobb, Georgia moderate, became President of the Convention, and since all agreed on a new federation, he appointed a committee which had little trouble drawing up a Provisional Constitution for the Confederate States of America. Principles of state rights were implicit in the existence of the Convention and were included in the constitution—but, interestingly enough, broad powers were given to the executive branch of the government and to the unicameral congress. Although the Provisional Government would last only until a permanent one could be erected in its place, under a Permanent Constitution, the Montgomery delegates were careful to provide adequate means of taxation in the Provisional Constitution as well as adequate means of raising and supporting military forces. Care also was taken to present a good face to the world and to make some concession to international opinion on slavery. The foreign slave trade was prohibited, but the possible admission of free states was not. Recognizing the commercial nature of Southern economy, the constitution contained provisions for regulation of commerce and freedom of navigation. And, to the satisfaction of many long-time Unionists, the new constitution borrowed most of its phraseology from the United States Constitution. In sum, the provisional charter avoided the excesses of the French Revolution, reflected none of the leveling tendencies which had been feared, and the Convention itself had no resemblance to the French National Assembly.

About the only point of similarity lay in the Convention's reluctance to go home. Once the Provisional Constitution had been drawn up and approved by the delegates on February 8, each state having one vote in ratification and in the new Congress, work progressed on a Permanent Constitution, which was soon approved and ratified to go into effect within a year. (*See Document No. 2.*) The Convention then proceeded with business and resolved itself into an electoral body to choose executives for the Provisional Government. And in the interest of saving time, the Convention also resolved into the first Provisional Congress.

Selection of Executives. As an electoral body, Congress displayed continuing moderation. Several prominent politicians were available for the presidency. Robert Barnwell Rhett of South Carolina had some claim to the post, since he had championed the Southern cause in Congress for many years and had tirelessly urged secession on his state and section. But he had urged always in the wildest terms, and his radicalism did not appeal to the Montgomery temper. For the same reason, Alabamian William Lowndes Yancey was not considered. Although one of the strongest voices for secession, an orator of peerless repute, a Southerner's Southerner, Yancey could not be counted on to charm the wavering border states. Alexander H. Stephens of Georgia, brilliant senator and political theorist, seemed a likely candidate, but he had been a late comer to secession—he was tarred with the brush of Unionism. Someone between extremes was needed, a man with experience and reputation.

A compromise candidate received the nomination: Jefferson Davis of Mississippi. There was much to recommend him. Born in Kentucky in 1808, son of a small farmer, Davis had been educated at Transylvania University and at the United States Military Academy. Following brief active service, he resigned the army to devote himself to the study of political theory. He went to Congress, led a Mississippi regiment with distinction in the Mexican War, and moved up to the United States Senate. His Senate tenure, interrupted for a few years while he served Franklin Pierce as Secretary of War, gave him maturity and high national reputation. If anyone could lay claim to Calhoun's mantle in 1860, Davis could. When Mississippi seceded, Davis delivered a brilliant farewell speech which stated the constitutional case for secession and deplored the necessity for ending a cherished confederation. Then he had gone back to his plantation. Davis hoped for peaceful separation, but more than most Southerners he knew the Northern temper and hence feared war. If he were needed by the South he wanted to lead an army in the field, but he sought no office, especially no political office. Because he was a moderate, because he had vast dignity and reputation and experience, he was unanimously elected President by the Congress on February 9, 1861.

The Vice-Presidency went to Alexander Stephens, partly to honor his past services, partly to honor Georgia, and partly as a sop to Union sentiment. To a man of boundless, burning ambition, of limitless personal esteem, the office must have been cheap consolation, but "Little Alec" accepted it. His is a tragic story of corroding frustration. In a short time he would drift away from Davis and the Confederacy, would join a junto of disaffected Georgians, and become virtually a traitor to the cause. Of all Confederates he is one of the most fascinating—a small, twisted man, body withered by disease, possessed by a brilliant mind. What he lacked in charm and grace, he had in wit and magnetism. He could have been one of the South's greatest assets.

Notified of his election, Davis left his Mississippi plantation for Montgomery, but he had many misgivings about the future. When he arrived on February 15, Montgomery greeted him with throngs and garlands and cheers. William L. Yancey pronounced that "the man and the hour have met," and the stirring scenes of enthusiasm encouraged Davis considerably. But still he knew the terrible problems facing the new nation and wasted little time on sentimental optimism. The views he would express in his inaugural address, the way he went about his task, told a lot about him.

Estimate of Davis. It was one o'clock in the afternoon of Monday, February 18, when Davis appeared before Congress and was escorted to the front portico of the Alabama capitol, newly designated the capitol of the Confederate States. A prayer was offered, then Davis stepped forward to speak. Those in the listening multitude who had an eye for omens were pleased—the day was cloudless, bright; the tall, ascetic looking speaker had a calm and determined air. Everything boded well for the new government. Everything but some of Davis' remarks.

The inaugural recited Davis' gratification at his election to the presidency, his high hopes for a Confederacy of the cotton states, the desire of the new government for domestic tranquillity and foreign friendship—and above all for peace with its neighbors. Secession, of course, had legal sanction, and had been employed not to undo the great work of the Founding Fathers but rather to preserve it. "We have changed constituent parts," said Davis, "but not the system of government." But he sounded a solemn warning: "If . . . passion or lust of dominion should cloud the judgment or inflame the ambition of [the United States] . . . we must prepare to meet the emergency and maintain, by the final arbitrament of the sword, the position which we have assumed among the nations of the earth." And he went on to list among immediate needs the speedy creation of the executive departments and preparations for raising military forces.

The man appreciated the moment, knew what to do to get started, but the speech had a legalistic ring, a preaching tone. Here was a flaw in Davis which time and testing never smoothed. Always he remained a cool, aloof, competent figure, talking in stilted phrase, straining for a bond with people which stayed just beyond his touch. His addresses, messages, declarations would inform, request, command, but never inspire, persuade, or ignite. Across Mason and Dixon's Line, Lincoln's language gained timeless luster. Davis[1] suffered the stricture of an exact mind. He had a warmth, an appeal, which only a few saw, and his inability to win friends finally divided him from the Confederate Congress, the people, and even from some of his own official family. Critics would say that he was a Chief Executive who was neither a chief nor an executive, but they were too harsh.

His virtues were impressive—dogged dedication, limitless capacity for hard work, knowledge of constitutional detail, military experience, unswerving loyalty to friends. But some of these virtues he carried to damaging excess, especially his dabbling in military matters, and his loyalty to friends even though they might be incompetents or political liabilities. Deficiencies came clear as the test of war increased. Davis interfered in command of armies too much, often to the detriment of military operations. A certain petty punctilio made him an unforgiving enemy— a quality which cost him the effective services of some of his better generals, such as P. G. T. Beauregard and Joseph E. Johnston. The same pettiness made him a stickler for presidential prerogative and a slave to detail.

But, in balance, the image of competence and courage which he projected as he delivered his inaugural was accurate. He proved to be the most courageous of Confederates, urged his country to fight almost beyond its endurance, stood the buffeting of slander, and stayed steadfast to the last. Few others could have done as well; probably none could have done better.

The Confederate Cabinet. While Congress toiled with initial legislation, Davis worked to build his cabinet, establish the government, find money, and prepare for war. Politics dictated that the President select his cabinet with an eye to state representation, party service, and ability. In a shrewd move, Davis gave the coveted post of Secretary of State to Robert Toombs of Georgia. Toombs' selection not only gave Georgia a second important position in the administration, but also recognized the fire-eater element. Toombs, who had wanted the presidency, almost spurned the secretaryship, but took it finally. A man of real ability and vast influence, he could be a dangerous foe, and Davis did well to win him to brief participation in the government. Toombs at length joined the army. His successors in the State Department were Robert M. T. Hunter of Virginia, and Judah P. Benjamin of Louisiana.

Since Davis feared war, he wanted to fill quickly the military posts in the cabinet. For Secretary of War he named Leroy Pope Walker. An important politician in Alabama Democratic ranks, Walker had been a leading voice in secession. He had some military experience as state militia general, but his selection came largely because of his party affiliation. In a few months he would resign, admitting to himself and everyone else that he had been a terrible administrator and had all but wrecked his department. After Walker came five other secretaries of war: Benjamin, George W. Randolph, G. W. Smith, James A. Seddon, and John C. Breckinridge—a long procession which indicated curious unrest in the War Department. Part of the trouble there stemmed from the President's penchant for being his own Secretary of War.

Fortunately for the Navy Department, Davis had little concern for ships or navies, beyond recognizing the need for some naval force. For the post of Secretary of the Navy, the President chose Stephen R. Mallory of Florida, and kept him in office through the war. Mallory's qualifications were better than most, since he had had experience as a member of the United States Senate Committee on Naval Affairs. And as the war progressed, it would be clear that Davis had found in Mallory the best man for a tough job. With almost no shipbuilding or engine works, Mallory would put warships at sea; would improve on the concept of the cruiser with the *Sumter, Alabama, Florida,* and on the concept of the ram with the *Stonewall*; would pioneer economic sea warfare with a concerted attack on the Union whaling fleet; would blaze a new trail with the ironclad *Virginia (Merrimac)*, whose famed battle with U.S.S. *Monitor* ushered in a new era in sea war. He also supported experiments with a submarine, the *H. L. Hunley,* and with various tropedo boats. Without resources, Mallory made the Confederacy a respected, even feared, power on the oceans.

Probably the most vital post in the cabinet, given the circumstances of the Confederacy, was Secretary of the Treasury. To it Davis named Christopher G. Memminger, South Carolina lawyer with a banking bent. Memminger's selection satisfied South Carolina with high office and brought to the cabinet a man of modest ability. History would serve Memminger ill, since the South failed to find money for the war. But it should be said in his behalf that he understood something of governmental finance, came to advocate stern tax measures in a time when taxes were most unpopular, and made use of loans, and forced credits—all in spite of his devotion to hard money. In the end his caustic personality, coupled with congressional refusal to adopt much of his program, doomed him to failure. In 1864, with floods of paper money cascading all over the Confederacy, with the public debt at an astronomical high, Memminger resigned under pressure and in his place came George A. Trenholm, another South Carolinian. Trenholm had vast international business interests, was a man of immense personal wealth, and Davis doubtless hoped that his wizardry in high finance would keep the South solvent. By 1864, of course, nothing could be done, but Trenholm tried.

The Post Office Department Davis saved as a reward to Texas for joining the Confederacy. A distinguished Texas jurist, John H. Reagan, consented to take the portfolio of Postmaster General. Usually a political sinecure, the office now had special problems in view of a requirement in the Confederate Constitution that the postal service should become self-sufficient. Reagan did a splendid job, fulfilled the constitutional obligation despite increasing difficulties, and remained in office throughout the war.

A new department appeared in Confederate cabinet organization—the Department of Justice, presided over by the Attorney General. Judicial advising, supervision of district attorneys, and management of some interior matters were among the Attorney General's duties. His responsibilities were heavily increased by the failure of Congress to create a Confederate Supreme Court. Davis' legal penchant made him acutely concerned with the Justice Department. His first choice for Attorney General was one of the South's most renowned lawyers—Judah P. Benjamin of Louisiana. Benjamin would become one of the most controversial Confederates and the President's continuing friendship for him would mean trouble for the entire Executive branch. Davis recognized Benjamin's brilliance and promoted him to the War Department in November, 1861, when Walker resigned. As War Secretary, Benjamin showed administrative talent but little awareness of military procedure. In 1862 he became Secretary of State, and had found his element. Once Benjamin left the Justice Department, it went to a series of replacements, all of them competent constitutional lawyers. Second Attorney General was Thomas Bragg of North Carolina, followed in March, 1862, by Thomas H. Watts (destined to be one of Alabama's war governors), then by another Alabamian, Wade Keyes, in October, 1863. The last Attorney General was another North Carolinian, George Davis, who took over in January, 1864.

Estimate of the Cabinet. History has condemned the Davis cabinet as an aggregation of mediocrities. The judgment is unfair and fails to consider available resources. How could the South, so another argument goes, present such poor men for administrative leadership after years of political maturity? One answer is, of course, that many Confederate politicians were barred from the government by their radicalism. Another is that the cabinet simply did not do as poorly as history implies. Davis' advisers were involved in managing the greatest war yet fought; old methods and means were inadequate to national needs. An administrative and civil service revolution occurred during the war in both North and South. Northern leaders had sufficient money and material to meet the crises of change; Southern leaders were forced to improvise, patch, and experiment. That they did enough to sustain a virtually total war for four years is some evidence of their ability to grow with responsibility.

Union-Confederate Relations. While at work forming his cabinet, Davis was also concerned with Union-Confederate relations. In response to a Congressional resolution, the President named a three-member commission to visit Washington and discuss matters of peaceful separation with Lincoln's government. Davis wrote Lincoln a conciliatory letter, introducing one of the commissioners and expressing hope for "friendly ties" between North and South.

Davis cherished few illusions, however, and at the same time pressed preparations for national defense. He asked Congress to permit the mobilization of regular and provisional troops and to appropriate funds to pay and equip land and sea forces. All matters of defense were taken under national control. States were directed to send military units to the field for Confederate use. Some militia troops could be retained by the states, but the national government should be allowed to call these into emergency service. Davis made it clear in his messages to Congress that there must be no doubt about the supreme authority of the Confederate government in all military matters. (*See Document No. 3.*)

Most pressing of military matters, aside from mobilization, was the peculiar condition of Federal forts in the harbors of Charleston, South Carolina, and Pensacola, Florida. The sovereignty of the Confederacy might well stand or fall on the issue of taking charge of these United States bastions. If the North retained them, the South could hardly claim direction of its own destiny. Diplomacy and politics demanded that the forts become Confederate property, as had arsenals and public installations in other parts of the Confederacy. For this reason, Davis charged the Washington commissioners especially to negotiate the matter of forts with Lincoln. The South would be patient but firm on this point. If negotiation failed, force might have to be used.

Military Preparations. No force could be used without arms and military equipment. Davis sought and received permission to purchase powder and arms from abroad and from the United States, and also to assume charge of all military equipment in the former United States arsenals and armories in all Confederate States. Regulations governing the raising and managing of an army were carried over from the United States, and the President received authority to put a provisional army in the field along with the regular army. Officers and men of the United States Army and Navy were encouraged to join Confederate forces, and officers usually were promoted one rank if they resigned their Yankee commissions and came South.

Congress shared Davis' concern with military measures, and gave him wide discretion in creating an army. He and the War Department achieved a minor miracle by marshaling almost 200,000 men in six months. These men were not always armed with the latest weapons, nor clothed in regulation uniforms, but with their rifles, shotguns, percussion and flintlock muskets, and assorted pistols and sabers, they were able to fight. A wave of patriotism swept the Southland and yielded many more men than the government could equip. Unfortunately, this crest of enthusiasm ebbed swiftly, and recruiting ever after would be a serious problem. But at least in mid-1861 the South had men enough for the threats that seemed ahead.

Finances. Part and parcel of the mobilization problem, of course, was the question of money. Armies and government required vast sums, and despite the myth of planter wealth, most of the Union's capital had long gathered in eastern financial houses—a fact which helped fan Southern hatred for the North. What could the Confederate government count on for money? At the outset

Memminger, like Albert Gallatin before him, underestimated the duration of the approaching crisis and called for light taxes, a fifteen million dollar loan, and the issuance of limited paper currency. The fundamental problem, naturally, was lack of money in the South. During the entire war the Confederacy found only about $27,-000,000 worth of specie. Consequently, paper money constituted the circulating medium. As it poured from Confederate presses its value decreased until, by 1865, even patriotic Southerners considered it a joke. Throughout the war, the Treasury Department, the President, and Congress wrestled constantly with money matters.

Initially, however, things looked fairly bright—the fifteen million dollar loan ultimately was oversubscribed, state loans were offered the government, and some United States bullion came from the New Orleans Mint and customhouse. Still, anyone with rudimentary business sense could see that domestic financial resources were thin. Foreign help would be needed. This seemed especially clear when over-all resources of the South were considered.

Confederate Resources. Should war come, the North possessed overwhelming advantages in manpower, money, ships, weapons, factories, and international prestige. Seven Southern states (eleven when Virginia, North Carolina, Tennessee, and Arkansas seceded; thirteen if the unseceded Confederate states of Kentucky and Missouri are included) would stand against twenty-three Northern states, would pit 9,000,000 people (3,500,000 of them slaves who were not military assets) against 22,000,000, and would rely on Lilliputian industry while the North organized the most industrialized war effort in history. The North had more than twice as many miles of railroad and a better managed and equipped agriculture, and most of the money. It had, too, diplomatic recognition around the world.

Optimists, and most Southerners were, could point to cotton as the Confederacy's white gold. The European demand for the Southern staple made foreign aid inevitable. Optimists could argue, too, that since the South had less to mobilize, manage, and direct, it might prepare for war more swiftly than the North, and perhaps win by speed what it might never win by force. In the final analysis, the South could count on hardy men, strong-willed women, and the desperation of home defense to sustain a war which could be won by simply not losing, by holding off invasion until the enemy grew weary or Europe intervened. Men, women, cotton, and hope were the South's sinews, and they proved stronger than any-one anticipated.

The Fort Sumter Crisis. It was Robert Toombs who warned an April cabinet meeting in Montgomery that if the South opened fire on Fort Sumter to assert its sover-eignty the greatest civil war in history would begin. But the problem of Sumter had ramifications so complex that war may have been the only solution. Lincoln's govern-ment refused to treat with the Confederate commission-ers; Lincoln never received them, and they concluded at length that Secretary of State W. H. Seward played a game of deceit while scheming to reinforce the fort and assert Yankee domination. One attempt to aid the fort by sending the *Star of the West* to Charleston with supplies ended when Palmetto batteries turned her back in Janu-ary. Lincoln, Davis, and South Carolina's Governor Francis Pickens played the Sumter game through Febru-ary and March with threats, innuendoes, promises, and lies until, at last, the Confederates developed a case of war jitters. Historians argue still whether Lincoln pursued a deliberate course of goading the Confederates into firing first. At any rate, an inexorable chain reaction had begun by early April. Confederate and South Carolina officials were then convinced that everything hinged on preventing reinforcements reaching Major Robert Anderson in Sumter. When rumors spread that a large relief expedi-tion at last had moved toward Charleston, Davis and his cabinet faced the agony of knuckling under or firing the first shot. They faced, too, the unknown factor of South Carolina, which might take matters in its own hands and flout the Confederate policy of moderation. On April 10, with cabinet approval, Secretary Walker sent a fateful order to Confederate General Pierre Gustave Toutant Beauregard, in Charleston. Demand surrender of the fort;

reduce it, if refused. The request was refused—all negotiations between Anderson and Beauregard having been conducted in the most gentlemanly manner—and at 4:30 A.M. April 12, 1861, a fiery red mortar shell arched across the harbor toward Sumter. (*See Documents Nos. 4 and 5.*) War!

2

THIN RANKS AND
SHORT RATIONS

Nature of War. Sumter answered a fundamental question: the Confederacy would either live or die by the sword. The people of the South were embattled, and as the war progressed they would find themselves embattled on a scale beyond their wildest imaginings. The war that Sumter started soon burst the bounds of previous American conflicts, made all experience obsolete, all precedent misleading. Small armies, commanded by individual generals, operating without national direction, were a thing of the past. North and South were on the brink of total war, and neither knew it or had any idea of how to wage it. Massive war came with massive populations, massive concentration of capital and industry, and with a revolution in management techniques. War was big business.

And because it was big business, it imposed special strain on the Confederacy—a nation innocent of large-scale business enterprise. The South would not only have to mobilize untapped resources, but also spawn a corporate effort. All Southern efforts would be conditioned by one terrible limitation: poverty. Poverty can ennoble; it can also frustrate. Often during the war Confederate military activities were frustrated by the grinding need for frugality, for a desperate husbanding of money, men, and supplies. Parsimony, far from being a sin, became a Confederate creed.

Problem of Manpower. Consider the question of manpower. When Rebels maintained that one Confederate could lick ten Yankees they were not boasting, simply stating a hard necessity. They were to be outnumbered most of the time, and this constantly confounded all recruiting problems. The illusion of sufficient manpower which Davis and Secretary Walker conjured by the middle of 1861 did not persist. When the three-months enlistees began to go home and the twelve-months volunteers talked of discharge, War Department officials realized that there was a good chance of Confederate ranks simply melting away. Volunteering seemed the only means of raising armies, aside from accepting the loan of state militia units. Both methods were tried, and shortly both proved inadequate.

State Troops. More trouble arose from state units than could have been anticipated. Governors who prated loudly of their zeal for the cause often reneged when called on to send militia to Confederate service. They were willing sometimes to lend their troops for limited use, but with the proviso of return to the state. Enrollment usually meant loss of the state units for the duration of the war, and many governors wanted their men for home defense.

Governor Joseph E. Brown of Georgia is the best example of recalcitrance. A fascinating man of Confederate history, Brown was brilliant and cocky. He waved a mesmeric wand over his legislature, and set himself against President Davis and the cause time and again. Presented with a loophole in manpower legislation, he commissioned—according to legend—10,000 second lieutenants in the Georgia militia and hence made them untouchable by Confederate authorities. He thought this a great coup, an example of his wit and local patriotism. Hindsight shows him instead an egotistical opportunist, willing to sacrifice a country for a trick. Fortunately for the South, not all state executives had such treasonable views. Governor John Milton of Florida, for instance, supported Confederate recruiting efforts and stripped the state of available men. His determination and the patriotic response of Floridians gave that least populated of Southern states the distinction of having the most men, per capita, in the Confederate army.

Decline of Volunteering. Even an optimist had to admit by the beginning of 1862 that regular methods of recruiting had failed. Fervid patriotism, which had sent so many to the armies in the summer of 1861, faded under the dreary discipline of camp life and the rigors of campaigning. Appeals of Southern belles to masculine spirit fell on wiser, deafer ears. Volunteers cautioned younger brothers to stay home (*See Document No. 6.*), and letters from camp and field told tearful tales of home-sickness, disease, and grinding boredom. War once had been a thing of glory but it had quickly tarnished.

Decline in volunteering could be tolerated in a nation with unlimited manpower resources, but in the Confederacy toleration was restricted by a cold statistic: there were only 1,280,000 white men between 15 and 50. Collapse of volunteering threatened destruction of the armies. How could a nation conceived in constitutionalism and dedicated to the proposition that all states were forever equal meet this crisis? It was a problem old as armies, one that had been met by royal decree, kidnapping, bribery, and punishment in other times and places. But America cherished the Minuteman tradition—the tradition of free men gladly doing battle for hearth and home. Americans had never been forced into national service—they had been obliged to do duty in the militia, but for limited time and in casual circumstance. There was nothing limited or casual about Confederate circumstance. Tradition had to be abandoned in face of necessity.

Conscription Begins. Davis took the first step on a long road toward centralization by advocating conscription. Many in Congress supported the President, were willing to wage hard war and to subordinate the states to Confederate authority. On April 16, 1862, by a majority of more than two to one, Congress passed the first national conscription act in American history. (*See Document No. 7.*) Surprisingly little resistance developed to the law. Confederate courts generally upheld its constitutionality, and the Southern people accepted the draft with far better grace than Northerners did a year later.

Imperfect in many respects, weakened by provisions allowing the hiring of substitutes and by an overgenerous exemption law, the draft act nonetheless served its initial purpose. By making all able-bodied white men between 18 and 35 subject to three years service, the evils of short-term enlistments were partially avoided and 154 regiments of twelve-months volunteers were kept with the colors. Unfortunately, Congress had to make concession to Southern individualism and state rights by allowing volunteering to continue. Hence the draft fell into disrepute; those who failed to volunteer were derided as slackers. "Conscript" became a dirty word, and men who went into the ranks through conscription were ostracized by "respectable" volunteers. Conscription should have been the sole recruiting system, of course, but Confederate circumstance made this impossible.

Consequently, the Administration and Congress were compelled to spend much time tinkering with the conscription laws and regulations. Trouble came naturally in the exemption business. Congress gave the Executive branch partial charge of regulating exemptions. This meant that many potential draftees who were more valuable at home could apply for Presidential exemptions. Applications had to be processed through the War Department, and inevitably inequities occurred. Protests flooded the War Office and public resentment increased. Class exemptions and substitutes caused a good deal of trouble, since they appeared to favor some elements of society over others.

"Twenty Slave Law." When it became clear that the first draft act would yield too few men, and that exemptions were not well designed, new laws were passed. The age limit was raised to 45 on September 27, 1862, and on October 11 many new classes were added to the exemption list. The exemptions included "one person as agent, owner or overseer, on each plantation of twenty negroes, and on which there is no white male adult not liable to military service." This infamous provision soon gave the name "twenty slave law" to the act, and aroused violent resentment as a prime example of class favoritism. It gave rise to the unhappy slogan "Rich Man's War and Poor Man's Fight" which plagued the Southern effort throughout the conflict.

Bureau of Conscription. High hopes were held for the second draft law. The Secretary of War expected it would bring at least 100,000 men to the ranks, but poor administration, passive resistance in several states, and continued volunteering tended to undercut the law's effectiveness. Clearly conscription could not be handled on a state or separate army basis. Some centralized program had to be instituted, and in order to enforce the second act the Secretary of War created a Bureau of Conscription in his department. Organized in January, 1863, as the agency in charge of all draft matters, the Bureau could have done much to conserve and manage the manpower pool. But poverty and consequent desperation once again thwarted the government's plans.

At the same time that the Bureau took over the business of finding, enrolling, and sending men to Camps of Instruction, the Army permitted General Braxton Bragg, commanding the Army of Tennessee, to set up his own Conscript Service. Under General Gideon J. Pillow, this army draft organization took charge of volunteers and draftees in Alabama, Mississippi, and Tennessee. Pillow pushed aside interference from War Department officers and did a thorough job of dragging in recruits. Men were swept into his net whether or not they had exemption certificates from other authorities, and screams of rage poured into Richmond from the Deep South. Severely reprimanded, Pillow sulked and Bragg fumed. Duplication and overlapping of effort obviously had to stop, but the urgent need of men for the Army of Tennessee in the summer of 1863 gave Pillow another chance. He and the Chief of the Bureau of Conscription in Richmond quarreled and competed. Pillow's efforts were more successful since he went after recruits with armed force, but he lost out finally to the War Department. The two conscription systems were obviously absurd, but were examples of the desperate makeshifts forced on the poverty-ridden South.

Desperate Measures. Deepening crisis spawned fiercer frenzy. When the gray army retreated from Gettysburg, when Vicksburg fell, when Georgia suffered the sear of Sherman, and when Lee's men were finally fastened in the Petersburg siege, all thought of careful management of men vanished. Every man for the ranks! This hysterical cry from the generals can be heard in any nation when a war is going badly, and usually it results in more harm than good. At a time when calm and careful husbanding of resources and uninterrupted war production might stave off disaster, shops, factories, railroads, mills, Navy Yards, are stripped of workers. Even if the comparatively few men gleaned from these sources do help fill the ranks, the supply lines will run dry, ammunition give out, food fail to reach the front, the economy collapse. So it was with the Confederacy on several occasions in late 1863, through 1864, and 1865. Conscription failed. More men were AWOL than were with the armies. General Lee, most respected soldier in the South, voiced a solemn warning that without more men "I fear a great calamity will befall us." War Department officials began to cancel all sorts of details and to dragoon the shop workers from ordnance and quartermaster plants.

Jefferson Davis did not yield to hysteria, and late in 1863 urged Congress to revamp the whole structure of conscription and exemption. (*See Document No. 8.*) On February 17, 1864, a new and comprehensive manpower law went into effect. The best of the draft acts, it came late but brought promise of success. Congress listened to some of the President's proposals and extended conscription to men between 17 and 50, provided that draftees from the 17-18 and 45-50 groups would go into reserve units for state defense, cut the class exemptions, and authorized the President to exempt and detail men certified as essential to war production. Designed to release men between 18 and 45 for field service who had been on interior details, the act drew hot fire from Yankee newspapers and from caustic General Ulysses S. Grant: the Rebels were robbing cradle and grave, were scraping the bottom of the manpower barrel.

Such criticism was inevitable but untrue; the act represented a rational attempt to centralize management of the Confederacy's manpower. For the first time the Administration had full authority to direct men to the front or to factories without endless red tape. But it came too late. By spring of 1864 resentment against conscription in Georgia, in parts of Alabama and Mississippi, and in the hill areas of North Carolina and Tennessee had hardened into hostility and armed resistance. Courts, politicians, state authorities conspired to flout the law, and the Bureau of Conscription reported only 15,820 men added to the armies between the first of January and the first of April. Possibly, thought the Bureau's chief, as many more men volunteered during the same period to escape the stigma of "conscript." In the same three months 26,000 men were exempted and 13,000 put on official details. Obviously, the Bureau had been more effective keeping men out of the army than getting them in. Complaints of felonious Conscript officers, illegal drafts, and brutish treatment of anyone who voiced doubt about the law, also indicated to the Administration that the Bureau was hurting the cause.

Conscript Bureau Abolished. In December, 1864, the War Department tried to overhaul the Bureau by instituting a self-inspection system. Officers sent to check on other Bureau officers soon were regarded as spies—which they were—and inspection became oppression. Davis made an effort to save the Bureau, although he knew its defects. But Congress, sensitive to popular resentment, abolished it early in 1865 and gave what remained of the drafting business to reserve officers in the various states. Conscription virtually ended in March, 1865, with the total exhaustion of the Confederate population.

Arming of Slaves. Nothing could overcome the defect of too few men. But when Lee's lines at Petersburg were decimated by staggering desertion, disease, and attrition, and other Confederate armies were ghost legions, the Conscript Bureau got the blame. In the agony of dying desperation, Lee, Davis, and Congress took up a suggestion which had been made earlier—arm the slaves. Opposition was fiery, of course, for this meant destruction of the South's "cornerstone," the sacrifice of a way of life. But independence loomed larger in many minds than slavery and if slaves were admitted to the ranks—albeit segregated ranks—the armies might be strengthened by half a million men. Congress, after long and grim debate, enrolled slaves in February, 1865. (*See Document No. 9.*) The great weakness in the slave enrollment act lay in the failure to grant freedom for service. Lee had urged that a plan of manumission go hand in hand with a draft, and Davis agreed. Congress, however, went far beyond anything a Southerner of 1861 could have anticipated in authorizing the use of Negroes as soldiers and ought not be too harshly criticized for stopping short of abolition. Negro troops never were a factor in the Southern war effort. A few were mustered in Richmond, but they were organized too late to make a difference.

Estimate of Conscription. Was conscription worth all the trouble it caused? Yes. It saved the Confederate armies at a critical point in 1862 and helped sustain them through the rest of the war. Despite defects and mal-administration, the conscription system drafted or forced enlistment of perhaps 300,000 soldiers in the Eastern Confederacy, and 120,000 west of the Mississippi. Since the South put a total of 850,000 men in the field, the Conscription Bureau, its appendages and competitors obviously did a remarkable job. They kept the ratio of Rebs to Yanks fairly steady at about 1 to 5—"good Confederate odds."

Cotton and Courage. Thin Rebel ranks were made thinner by short rations. Poverty in manpower was matched by poverty in every other resource. Statistically, of course, the South could not match its adversary in anything save cotton and courage. Cotton could conceivably be used for clothing, but courage seemed a poor substitute for bread. Ardent Rebels argued at the beginning that a nation of farmers never would go hungry— a euphemism belied by Lee's gaunt few at Appomattox.

Army Food Shortages. But the Confederacy was an agricultural nation, an area of abundant land and long growing season. How could it go hungry? It went hungry first because planters hated to stop growing cotton—a staple ingrown in the Southern mind and economy. When the Confederate government urged the curtailment of cotton production and the sowing of food crops in a sort of voluntary cotton embargo, many planters ignored the plea. They heeded it only when they themselves needed food and then it was too late. The armies starved, too, because of mismanaged procurement and distribution of military supplies.

Logistics. The science of getting men, equipment, and supplies together at the right time and place is known as "logistics." Now the heart and soul of military thought, logistics in 1860 was in its infancy. Total war brought it to rapid and peculiar maturity in the Confederacy. Generally defined as the science of managing a nation's resources for war, it became in the South a sort of economic sleight-of-hand. Since money and all supplies were scarce, logistics grew into a science of makeshift, a matter of finding substitutes for necessities, of patching the unpatchable. All Confederate supply men—commissaries, quartermasters, ordnance officers, surgeons, engineers— were adept in the science of makeshift and worked minor miracles finding and issuing food and equipment.

Impressment. But there was just so much to be had. Food shortages by late 1862 helped drive prices up astronomically, and when the army went on short rations, government authorities began to impress, or commandeer, what they needed. Impressment proved more unpopular even than conscription. It flouted the sanctity of property, took a man's produce, livestock, his bread and meat —it was the ultimate invasion of personal liberty and the acme of centralization. Theoretically, military men were to pay fair prices for impressed property, but callous or spurious officials often ignored the theory. Frequent complaints of outright seizure, or payment in despised "certificates of indebtedness" (a government promissory note), damaged the reputation of the Administration and made the whole process intolerable.

Congress tried to correct some evils with a general act regulating impressment in March, 1863. (*See Document No. 10.*) Infractions continued. Even patriotic citizens resented the practice, and when they joined in mass evasion of the law in 1864, morale had virtually collapsed.

Estimate of Impressment. Unpopular as it was, impressment was essential; it virtually alone supplied the Army and Navy after mid-1863. By then Confederate currency poured from the presses at a rate exceeded only by rising prices and the government simply could not afford to buy supplies on the open market. A feeble administration effort had been made to encourage voluntary price-fixing when it became clear that taxation did not sufficiently cut the amount of money in circulation. Confederate price schedules were published in various cities, and Army, Navy, and public officers were expected to purchase supplies at these rates. (*See Document No. 11.*)

But producers rejected the ludicrously low official prices and sold only to private consumers. Ruinous costs or impressment—these were the alternatives. Impressment probably did more than anything else to divorce the people from the government, but without it the war would have been lost much sooner.

Nationalization of Industry. Impressment proved only one facet of the procurement dilemma. Government policy dictated that Army and Navy officers do their best to let contracts for their needs and impress only when the contracts failed. Sound in principle, the contract system broke down in practice. Private armories, mills, shops, mines, and furnaces—works of all kinds—were unable to keep going under the stress of rising costs, dearth of skilled and unskilled labor, chronic shortage of materials and tools. Faced with bankruptcy and breach of contracts, private owners often had to sell out to the government. All supply branches of the War and Navy Departments were forced into manufacturing, and by 1864 large segments of Confederate industry had been nationalized.

To prevent the central government taking over everything, some states moved to nationalize their own industries. North Carolina, for instance, became a textile empire. Over one-half of Confederate textiles were made in the Tar Heel state by 1864, and Governor Zebulon Vance took charge of production in order to keep Davis' agents away. So thoroughly did he manage state plants that when Lee's starved, ragged few reached Appomattox, there were 92,000 new uniforms stored in North Carolina—waiting to be issued to North Carolina troops!

Distribution of Supplies. Supplies once obtained, by impressment or otherwise, had to be processed and sent to the armies. Processing often involved packaging or sacking, and materials for both were scant. Lumber for boxes could be had, but wrapping paper was saved with fierce parsimony and twine almost disappeared. The most suitable grain sacks were made of burlap, but burlap became so rare that in its place Confederates used cotton "Osnaburg" in great quantities.

Once processed or packed, supplies had to be stored or

shipped. Warehouse space grew scarcer as more was
taken for military goods and as the enemy occupied large
Confederate cities. Government rents soared, and sometimes the Army impressed buildings to save money.
Quartermaster, ordnance, and commissary officials relied
heavily on the depot system after mid-1863. By establish-
ing numerous field supply points which could be re-
plenished from major depots, Army and Navy officers
gained government owned storage space, control over
stock, and flexibility in distribution.

Confederate Railroads. The whole business of logistics hinged on transportation. And logistics had been
transformed by the advent of the railroad. Trains made
possible quick movement of mass armies and mountains
of supplies, the collection and efficient distribution of
natural resources. They made possible total war, and led
one Confederate general to a modern paraphrase of
Napoleon: "Railroads are at one and the same time the
legs and the *stomach* of an army."

As in everything else the South lagged behind in railroads. At the outset the Confederate States could boast
only 9,000 miles of track, compared with the North's
22,000 miles. But the disparity in shops, repair facilities,
and engine works put the Confederacy still further behind. Southern railroad companies purchased their loco-
motives, cars, and track from the North, sent their equipment to Northern shops for refurbishing, and depended
on Northern capital for railroad expansion. Only two
iron works in the Confederacy could cast boiler plate or
locomotive wheels, trucks, or track. And these works
could function only with a supply of iron.

Confederate railroad men worked wonders with almost
no resources. Faced with multiple short lines, differing
gauges in the large cities, few tools or materials, limited
rolling stock, Rebel railroaders contrived to keep trains
going—they tore up useless lines and used the track on
military roads; they burgled cars and facilities where they
could; filched as much equipment as possible from the
enemy; patched worn cars and engines until they literally
fell apart. Toward the last, Confederate engines crept
along at glacial speed lest they jump worn-out, weaving

tracks, and frequently did stall or overturn. But they still were running right at the end—no small achievement.

Confederate officials never devised a satisfactory system of railroad management. Hampered by state rights and laissez-faire theories, the government tried to work through private owners. But the problems which plagued all Confederate contractors especially plagued the rail lines. Men and material grew incredibly scarce. Parts had to be made in shops that did not exist—costs rose drastically. Some Confederate railroads asked for government management, but the Administration never went that far. Scattered attempts were made to give over-all direction to railroads: regulations were issued governing Confederate freight and emergency impressment, schedules were devised, an Iron Commission sought metal. But private enterprise had to limp along as best rickety engines, wobbling wheels, and undulating tracks would permit. Government control would have helped to keep trains in operation and out of the hands of speculators. Food, ammunition, and other vital necessities sometimes were ignored by rail officials for more lucrative private business, and the government should have intervened. In general, the main arteries of the Confederate transport system stayed open but congested; coagulation was chronic. The railroads can be credited with almost sustaining the long and remarkable Rebel war effort.

Mules and Wagons. To a lesser degree that effort also depended on other kinds of transportation. Traditionally mules and wagons were the mainstays of army transport. Mules grew scarce in the wartime South; wagons scarcer. When possible, horses replaced mules, and wagons were rebuilt, coaxed, and wheedled as fervently as trains. Impressment of horses and wagons provided barely adequate field transportation. Remount depots and quartermaster repair shops worked wonders of resuscitation and salvage.

River Transportation. Riverboats had long plied the hundreds of rivers, creeks, and streams of the South. These waterways provided natural lines of communication and commerce in every southern state, lines which had been used long before roads or railroads. But the shallow and short coastal feeders were of small use and the large rivers became invasion routes for Yankee monitors and gunboats. The coast and inland waters were the Confederacy's Achilles' heel—a fatal front defended occasionally by scattered land forces and the enfeebled Confederate Navy. An obvious transportation asset became a tragic military liability.

Industrial Expansion. Such a long list of deficiencies paints a distorted picture of the Confederacy's condition. True, it began poor, became poorer, and died broke. But during the war, incredible things were done to prop up the economy—things which tell much about strength born of devotion and nurtured in desperation.

In the beginning there were almost no factories in the South. Some textile mills were strewn over North Carolina, Virginia, and a few other states; some iron deposits were known in Alabama; some furnaces existed in parts of the South, but only one heavy machinery plant existed —the Tredegar Iron Works in Richmond. Every industrial advantage lay with the enemy.

Largely due to the efforts of a Pennsylvania-born organizational genius, General Josiah Gorgas, Confederate Chief of Ordnance, the South girded until it became something of a small industrial power. Ordnance works were established in Texas, Arkansas, Louisiana, Mississippi; at Selma, Alabama (employing over 3,000 civilians); at Atlanta, Augusta, Columbus, and Macon, Georgia; at Fayetteville, North Carolina, and at Richmond. These plants made the Confederacy self-sufficient in gunpowder, and almost self-sufficient in ammunition and arms. They were not big enough nor were there enough of them to give Rebel troops equipment equal to that of the affluent Yankees. But these plants were adequate to an effort which exhausted resources, which yielded up unknown treasures of minerals and makeshifts, which gleaned window weights for bullets and church bells for cannons. Weak and mismanaged as the Confederate economy is reported, it maintained the most thorough mobilization of modern times.

Estimate of Confederate Effort. Ranks were thin and rations short—more men could have been hauled into the armies, more food could have been forced to the front. But as it was, the South put three-fourths of its total military population in the field, spent all its money, wore out its machinery, and sustained 350,000 casualties. No other people offered so much, suffered so fiercely, lost so completely.

3

DIXIE LAND

Role of Confederate Women. Women always have to be reckoned with—Southern women especially. Generally, they have been more bloodthirsty than Southern men. They were during the Civil War. Patriotism ran high in the beginning; men flocked to enlist and drive back the blue invader. Those who went usually carried with them some token of a lady's love—a handkerchief with a bygone tear, a Bible with stilted inscription, a book of proper verse, a garter with lusty motto. Men who did not go—for reasons or for qualms—felt the special chill of female ostracism.

Better far than bayonets were Southern belles as recruiters. Ladies had long been placed on pedestals in the Southern tradition; they represented the goodness and virtue of a society conceived in gentility and dedicated to the proposition that breeding had its just rewards. Women symbolized the family, were the custodians of lineage. Even women of the "lower classes" received the homage and protection of "gentlemen." They were the weaker sex, hence curiously above and beyond the dailiness of life.

If the Southern attitude toward women seemed absurd to many Northerners, and especially so to Europeans, it was neither absurd nor artificial to Southern men. They tended the duties of chivalry as an act of faith and understood it to include the sanctity of home against all comers, particularly Yankees.

An item missed by many Southern gentlemen; women were not out of things. They adjusted to their pedestals, and behind facades of silks, linens, hoops, and fans contrived the lives of men. Home and fireside they would defend as they could. So they sent men to battle with waves of patriotic frenzy, coaxed, goaded, wheedled, persuaded. If some men felt a certain irritation at such blatant feminine desire to be rid of them, most nonetheless accepted fate and went.

Those who conformed to petticoat patriotism were rewarded in love and panoply. In every town and county, ladies lavished their best silks on banners and tassels for local companies. "Davis Guards," "Richmond Grays," "Invincibles," "Yankee Catchers," "Gideonites," "Wild Cats"—almost every unit that marched away to martial airs and tender smiles, carried a flag made by dainty hands and presented by a lissome lass who spoke hopefully of safe return and wrathfully of the enemy. So called "elite" units, such as the famed Washington Artillery of New Orleans—in which the most prominent families were represented at the lowest ranks—went off to camp after proper and impressive "levees," to which ranking politicians and generals came.

When gaiety gave way to gore, when the wounded streamed from a hundred fields and men were maimed and broken by battle, women did not quail. They remained the steadiest Rebels. Ladies of all lots went from plantations, homes, squalid hovels, to hospitals. They had not before been exposed to the horrors of the wounded, had not been expected to see men dying in droves. But as Clara Barton's dedicated corps mended the broken blue men, so countless gray ladies cared for their Rebels. Stories of quiet heroism at thousands of Confederate bedsides are legion. Southern belles were made of sturdy mettle.

Ladies became more essential to the Confederate effort than anyone could have expected at the outset. The changing status of women told more forcefully than almost anything else the upheaval in Southern life wrought by the war. From relative obscurity, from fabled shelter, Southern women went not only to hospitals, but also to munitions factories, quartermaster shops, government offices. They filled hundreds of men's jobs, hence con-

tributing vitally to the war. A few male impersonators
fought in the field; spying became a feminine art. Despite
later attempts to reëstablish the old order, women were
never to resume the same condition of abstraction as
before the war.

At times a few of them grew weary—and small wonder.
Many found themselves responsible for large plantations
while all their men were at the front. Slaves often grew
indolent and some restive in the absence of masters;
overseers, too, took advantage of their sudden power.
Women on small farms frequently had to plow and pick
cotton, sow and harvest food. Marketing crops imposed
terrible burdens on them, for many had no slaves and
could not afford hired help. Inflation priced commodities
out of range of soldiers' wives, who had to eke out a
living on part of an infantryman's eleven Confederate
dollars per month.

Family Problems and Desertion. Clothing grew
scarce and expensive. About the only thing that saved
style-conscious Southern belles was an informal agreement by which many of them forswore wearing anything
other than homespun until the war's end. Even so, real
privation came. Rumors of families without winter clothing and without food made the armies uneasy and when
rumors were confirmed in letters from home, desertion
became a serious problem. Men went AWOL to take care
of their families, often intending to return when planting
was done or crops were harvested. But starvation, penury,
and hunger were potent Yankee allies.

Morale. Penury and privation worked an insidious
decay. Morale had been higher in the South at the beginning than in the North, higher perhaps than in any previous American war. But failure of the government to keep
the reasons for fighting in the public mind, plus the price
spiral, the collapse of Confederate currency, scarcity of
any luxuries at all, the grinding blockade which shut the
South off from trade, brought weariness and want. Add
the cold fact of military defeat and patriotism lost its
verve. High in the hopeful days of 1862, when Rebel
armies stormed into the enemy's country, morale sagged
in the hard winter of that year, climbed again in spring,

dropped with Stonewall Jackson's death after Chancellorsville, and broke sharply with the twin disasters of Gettysburg and Vicksburg in July, 1863.

But Confederates were dogged, and hope revived with the victory at Chickamauga, Georgia, in September. Little good news came in 1864, but in face of retreat and erosion of their country, most civilians almost matched the armies in devotion. With summer came unremitting disaster: Grant struck hard at Lee and toward Richmond; Sherman scorched Georgia and wrenched Atlanta from the Army of Tennessee. Brief expectations of miraculous deeds from General John B. Hood and that same heroic army in Tennessee were dashed by abject defeat at Nashville in December, and Sherman began his ruinous scourge through the Carolinas.

Everything centered on Lee. Nothing else lasted, but his Army of Northern Virginia hung on, a band of iron skeletons bucklered by a nation's hope and a general's genius. With his army still holding Richmond, Rebel optimism revived at the end with a brief, burning intensity. Desperation doubtless brought it back, for it had no foundation in fact.

State of the Economy. By mid-1864 the economy had disintegrated. An agrarian nation forced into industrialization, the Confederacy had done surprisingly well, but poverty and adversity took their toll. Most Southern capital had been in land and slaves when the war began. Liquid funds were limited and largely mortgaged to Northern banks and bankers. This close connection between Northern and Southern business, between Northern money and Southern slavery, gave some hope that war could be averted. War would disrupt business, and, hence, businessmen were not warmongers. Secession might preserve the sanctity of contracts, but war would wipe out obligations. Northern commercial elements became moderates on the Southern question and conservative patriots. But the fact remained that they had most of the South's money when the war came.

True, a few banks in larger Confederate cities boasted respectable assets, but far from enough to support a national war economy. And stagnation of commerce, inevitable after Lincoln's proclamation of blockade in April, spelled rapid ruin to planters, merchants, and bankers alike unless domestic trade and war industry rose rapidly and the government devised a sound money system.

Early Financial Measures. Christopher Memminger, harried Secretary of the Treasury, soon realized the parsimony of his early financial program and recommended a $50,000,000 loan in May, 1861, along with a $15,000,-000 direct tax and an import duty of twelve and a half percent. At the same time, and fatefully, he admitted the inadequacy of the $1,000,000 issue of treasury notes in February and urged printing another $20,000,000.

Unfortunately, the first $15,000,000 loan offered in February, though finally oversubscribed, lagged for months because of money scarcity in the South. To stimulate the second one among the planters, Congress tried a novel experiment: the Produce Loan. This permitted planters and farmers to pledge the income from unharvested produce as security for the new bonds. At first highly vaunted and popular, the Produce Loan finally failed. Farmers feared they might be victimized by low prices. When Memminger reported in July that Confederates showed an alarming coolness toward government bonds and loans, Congress weakly authorized another $100,000,000 in treasury notes.

Income Tax and Tax-in-Kind. Memminger knew, as did Davis and many in Congress, that taxes were the heart of any wartime financial program, and vital in curbing inflation. But taxes were never happily received, especially in the South with its customary affection for no government interference. Nothing came harder to a Congress steeped in state rights dogma than stern national taxation. Urged by Memminger and the president, Congress proved it could take some bitter medicine and do difficult deeds to save the currency. On April 24, 1863, it passed a general levy, stiffer and tighter than anything before, and included in the act a provision for an income tax which ranged as high as fifteen percent on sums above $10,000. An income tax came extremely hard; it represented a forced contribution to the government without even the slight consolation of bonds or interest-bearing notes. And it proved what many suspected: the government grew increasingly despotic and dictatorial. But Congress did more.

In the same act it levied a profits tax on farm produce, and on certain other natural resources, and assessed a contribution by farmers and planters of one-tenth their annual yield of foodstuffs. This "tax-in-kind," as it came to be known and hated, involved the government in serious collection and transportation problems. Agents of the tax-in-kind—TIK men—many of whom were the vilest frauds, found it easier to handle produce from farms and plantations close to railroads; hence the same farms were called on time and again, while those in remote areas might never see a TIK man.

The tax-in-kind alienated everybody. Farmers thought it discriminatory class legislation; non-farmers thought it gave a special advantage to planters. But unpopular, unfair, unreasonable, and unevenly collected, the tax-in-kind was vital—it brought in food when money collapsed and when the government schedule prices became laughing-stocks. Like impressment, the tax-in-kind was an evil necessity which harmed the cause and yet sustained it.

Problems of Paper Money. But these expedients failed to stop inflation. Congress could never bring itself to put real iron into tax collecting nor to halt the ruinous flood of paper currency. Wreckage of the economy would have come had the Confederate government alone issued cascades of paper, but it came sooner when states added theirs to the total. Congress never declared Confederate currency the sole medium of exchange and so fostered competition with state monies and bonds. In fact, as prices soared and Confederate notes grew worthless, many people preferred state money.

Memminger desperately planned partial repudiation in mid-1863 when he advocated a funding act to take roughly a third of the total currency out of circulation. This act, grudgingly passed in February, 1864, had complicated provisions for turning in old money for new in various places at various times; it had large loopholes and such loose provisions for taxing land and slaves—the South's best assets—that it did little good. A brief honeymoon of lower prices, right after the law went into effect, soon ended and prices went still higher. In theory, funding should have reduced the outstanding $973,000,000 by $300,000,000, but Memminger never discovered how much money actually was called in. This much all could see: funding did not halt inflation. Failure of such stringent measures as multiple taxes and repudiation brought Memminger into violent disrepute, and in the summer of 1864 he resigned.

George A. Trenholm replaced him, but came too late. By mid-1864 Confederate credit had evaporated at home and abroad. Ridiculously small efforts at borrowing from Europe had failed; the famed Erlanger Loan produced much less than expected, and Confederate agents in foreign parts were forced to rely on cotton pledged for delivery through the blockade.

Value of Confederate Money. Some economists have argued that Memminger could have saved his country, and incidentally his job, had he based Confederate currency on cotton or tobacco—Southern staples of steady supply and rising world value. Perhaps, but the Southern people instinctively valued their money in gold, hence robbing themselves of their own special specie. Trenholm could not reverse an old error. He did everything he could, but faced waning confidence in the cause, and without public confidence, currency is worthless.

When Lee's remnants marched to stack arms at Appomattox, a Confederate dollar was virtually without gold value. Gold ratio, however, had little to do with the utility of Rebel currency. Since mid-1863, Confederate notes had dropped in value, but as long as Southern citizens used them the cause lasted. When all hope went, so went the money. Congress must be blamed for poor financial planning and essentially cowardly taxation. Had heavy levies been enacted and ruthlessly collected early in the war, prices might have been kept lower and the nation supplied with sound money. Memminger, Davis, and many members often preached sternly to Congress about the paralyzing effects of paper money based on nothing—but once started, the presses could not be stopped.

Failure of Financial Programs. Davis is partly to blame, for he failed to give effective and consistent executive leadership in money matters, and clung too long to

Memminger after Congress had lost faith in the Secretary. Still, both the Secretary and the President knew what needed to be done and talked a good program—that Congress failed to enact it brought on the crises aptly described by a modern student of Confederate history, Charles W. Ramsdell: "The resort to irredeemable paper money and to excessive issues of such currency was fatal, for it weakened not only the purchasing power of the government but also destroyed economic security among the people. In fact, there seems to be nothing vital that escaped its baneful influence." Still, in sum, Davis, treasury officials, and Congress deserve praise for what they did with what they had: few, if any, others could have carried on a total war for four years with only $27,000,-000 worth of hard money.

Deterioration of Economy. Inflation and myriad monies were part of the over-all economic deterioration which disrupted all elements of Confederate society. Collapse of trade must be ranked with inflation as a potent enemy of survival. Always the South depended on exporting its cotton to Northern markets, thence to world marts. An agricultural nation could hardly hope to exist with mercantile avenues closed. The blockade dealt dual mortal blows to the Confederacy. It choked foreign commerce, and slowed domestic trade. Since Southern life hinged on cotton's success, stifling of cotton gagged the entire economy. Internal business activity dwindled in proportion to cotton income and scarcity of commodities.

Widespread Scarcity. Everything people wanted was scarce and expensive. Ladies suffered privation of fashions; most Rebels at home suffered mild to severe starvation and were often forced to shameful scrambling, even theft, for such necessities as medicine. All medical supplies were desperately needed by the military, were listed as contraband by Union cruisers, and any found within Confederate borders went to impressment officers or to heartless speculators—quinine, practically a staple in malaria country, sold for as much as $100 an ounce in 1864.

Commonplace things became vital. Salt, which had been easily available, disappeared from the scene—and without it planters, farmers, merchants, army commissaries, could not preserve meat. Efforts to condense salt from sea water proved haphazard and often were foiled by marauding Federal ships. There were only two reliable sources of salt: the wells at Saltville in southwestern Virginia, and the impressive rock salt mines at Avery Island in southern Louisiana. The Louisiana mines were captured in 1863. Prices of salt skyrocketed during the war, ranging from eighty cents a bushel in 1861 to $30 in 1863 and $80 to $100 in 1865.

Meat, too, grew rare. Army needs were constant and were first supplied. Herds of cattle, hogs, livestock of all kinds attracted impressment officers, and complaints were frequent that many farms had been stripped of all meat, despite orders to leave something for home use. Cattle had special value, since hides provided leather for harness, soles, machine belting, saddles, bridles, cartridge boxes, and myriad other items.

The Civil War was a conflict of iron and leather, of clangor and creak. And when tanneries ran low on hides, Southerners devised remarkable substitutes. Government factories experimented with machine belting made of cotton cloth stitched in multiple thicknesses and soaked in linseed oil: it worked. Harried quartermasters hit on the novel idea of shoes with wooden soles and canvas tops —satisfactory, legend has it, to all but the wearers!

Behind the lines civilians, too, grew expert at devising substitutes for everything. Cotton cloth, of course, was made to do things silks and satins had traditionally done. Folk remedies replaced scarce medicines; the Surgeon General's Office even published an herbal to guide people in home cures and makeshift recipes. (*See Document No. 12.*)

Outlandish concoctions appeared in the guise of coffee. Parched ground corn seems to have been the most common Rebel "coffee," though hardly palatable. Molasses replaced sugar; cornmeal, flour. Drab country fare— sweet potatoes, peas, cornbread, and sowbelly—became the Confederate gourmet's delight.

Confederate Humor. Through 1863-1865, years of demoralization and deprivation, the Confederacy kept a saving sense of humor. When speculation, taxation, depredation, nakedness, and hunger pressed in from all sides, laughter was the only recourse. During the siege of Vicksburg, for instance, a mock menu of the "Hotel de Vicksburg" boasted mule tail soup, mule roast, cotton berry pie, and Mississippi River water, "vintage 1492, very inferior." A good deal of doggerel verse aimed humorous barbs at the Yankees, and some fair poetry caught the absurdity of war. Theatergoers in Richmond, Atlanta, Charleston, virtually any large city, were treated to countless plays, skits, and songs lampooning Lincoln, Davis, Uncle Tom, or some hapless Union general. Bill Arp probably ranked as the best Confederate humorist, but he had many compatriots.

Soldiers are rich sources of earthy humor, and Johnny Reb was no exception. He had boundless capacity for ribald jokes and songs, for devilish and sometimes ghoulish pranks. Almost every semi-permanent army camp sported a humorous magazine or occasional paper—crude forerunners of *Stars and Stripes!*

Social Life. Humor lasted because life was not all bad, and because the natural Southern need for gaiety was never exterminated. Mary Boykin Chesdnut, in her charming and witty *Diary from Dixie,* tells of the frequent dances, balls, parties, gatherings of all sorts that brightened Richmond's wartime gloom. On rare occasions some of the storied lavishness could be glimpsed in a jealously hoarded damask tablecloth, in a furtive bottle of vintage champagne, in a succulent roast pig or turkey. But almost as much fun was had at the far more frequent "starvation parties," where substitute menus were featured and watery toasts quaffed. Similar entertaining occurred outside of Richmond, even in remote areas and on lonesome plantations. Southerners have always been gregarious and impending doom added a special poignance to the trait.

Festivities gave brief release from war, and all occasions were seized on as excuses for parties, dinners, or visiting. In the larger cities military heroes were lionized in a hectic social whirl; visiting dignitaries were duly watered and dined. And when Johnny Rebs went home on leave, every house, farm, and plantation bustled with cooking, baking, polishing, and party "doins." The thousands of "refugees" whose tragic migrations mirrored Yankee inroads, found the latchstring usually out, although they often tried the patience of Southern hospitality.

Religious Spirit. Southerners also had a solemn side. And Confederates were not only serious but also sentimental—for the 1860's were sentimental years. Natural sentiment and solemnity made the Confederate people deeply religious. Many looked to God for deliverance from the terrible afflictions of Civil War. Religious leaders strove to meet the challenge of such abiding faith. Several Protestant denominations showed Southern nationalism by separating from Northern brethren in the ante bellum years, and ministers joined zealously in preaching the Confederate cause. Pulpits became main bulwarks of Southern patriotism; from them came fiery exhortations to take up Gideon's sword and smash the Philistines, to gird in God's armor for a Holy War against Satan's blue myrmidons.

A cause so virtuous, for which so many devout had given their lives, surely would win the favor of the Old Testament's Jehovah. And for a time it seemed so. Ministers exulted to their congregations, to camp meetings among the troops, that God had showed His mercy in victory after victory in 1861 and 1862. Lee's Army, partly led by Deacon Stonewall Jackson, was likened to Cromwell's New Model Army—an aggregation of Christian crusaders.

But time brought defeat and hunger and disease and wholesale death. Had God deserted the Confederacy? By late 1863, after the disasters of Vicksburg and Gettysburg, many at home thought so and, hence, deserted God. But in the armies the question worked a strange and wonderful alchemy. Hard gray men, stalwarts of the fiercest campaigns, turned to the Almighty when too few of them were left to battle longer alone. Waves of revivalism swept the armies; chaplains found themselves preaching to larger congregations than ever they had seen, and reported ecstatically that conversions ran to thousands. These outpourings of religious fervor among the soldiers were chronicled with feeling by Confederate chaplain J. William Jones in his *Christ in the Camp*.

Songs of Sentiment. The shock of defeats during the last years forced many Southerners to think of death. Sons, husbands, brothers, lovers were slain in windrows on countless fields; disease took thousands at home. Death stalked the ravaged Southland without respite; the Reaper took relentless toll. A morbid preoccupation with death, added to natural sentimentality, colored much of the work of Confederate artists, writers, and musicians. For every humorous verse, play or song, there were three or four somber ones. Listeners could indulge their melancholy to the hilt when they heard "Lorena," "All's Quiet on the Potomac," "Dear Mother, I've Come Home to Die," or "We Shall Meet, but We Shall Miss Him," and there were a hundred more. Musical tastes shifted from enthusiastic demand for martial and patriotic airs such as the unofficial anthem, "Dixie," early in the war, to fascination with cadenced dirges toward the end.

Novelists. No Rebel novelist wrote an *Iliad*. War seemed to parch the talents of the best Southern writers, and few fictional works appeared. Among those few, the best remembered is *Macaria: or, Altars of Sacrifice,* by the famed Alabama novelist Augusta Jane Evans Wilson. A chill and cheerless tale of patriotic immolation, it gave courage to many readers and nerved them to further selflessness for the South. But the larger names among the South's writers produced little to recall. William Gilmore Simms confined his restless pen to a few bad verses and some political propaganda.

Poets. Poets did the memorable work of the Confederate era. Among the most famous were Henry Timrod and Paul Hamilton Hayne, and both were fired to art by war. In his haunting love song to the South, "Ethnogenesis," Timrod caught the spirit of Confederate nationalism, and in his "A Cry to Arms," he took a stirring stand for Dixie. Hayne felt the agony of wholesale slaughter with the poet's special nerve. He spoke the lament of a people in "Our Martyrs." But in sadness he felt, too, the exultant stir of battle and gave it searing life in "Scene in a Country Hospital." (*See Document No. 13.*)

Artists. Wartime artists almost always took bits of the conflict for their themes. Some of the finest sketch work limned soldier life in camp and battle. Adalbert Volck's camp scenes are valuable historical sources, as are the numerous sketches of Louis Montgomery, soldier in the Washington Artillery. Painting also reflected the

sentimental Confederates on many a large and maudlin
canvas. Perhaps the most famous Southern war painting
was William Washington's somber group gathered for
"The Burial of Latané." But despite much solid effort,
Rebel artists did not rise to war's challenge and were
mainly mediocre.

The People. Confederate creativity flourished especially in the realm of the spirit. Grinding poverty, steady
erosion of the Southland, at length a dying country, tried
the people to the utmost. Many, of course, broke to mean
selfishness and sometimes treason. But others stayed steady
and grew in soul as they wasted in body—those countless
thousands of women, children, old men, soldiers, and
the many faithful slaves who lasted to the end. A look at
the sufferance behind the lines makes it clear that whatever else may be said of the Confederacy, the people
ennobled the cause.

— 4 —

THE ILLUSION OF KING COTTON

Diplomacy is that branch of human endeavor which has for its object the destiny of nations. Some consider it an art, others a game, still others a system of deceit. Whatever the label, diplomacy's practitioners strive for high stakes—war, peace, international position.

By definition, then, a diplomat is a man of vision, intelligence, knowledge, rare tact, steady nerve, boundless charm, and cold calculation—a consummate conniver. But few diplomats can boast such talents. Most of them are solid, honest career men who vaguely abhor cupidity, or bold, gambling amateurs who suffer the defect of self-confidence. Diplomacy is a subtlety best understood by veteran knaves and venerable nations.

The United States had almost no diplomatic maturity in 1861; its statesmen were amiably joshed as typical Brother Jonathans. But the United States had more experience and more prestige than the Confederate States. The new nation began its quest for international status with the limitations of ignorance and the certainties of youth.

Basic Diplomatic Strategy. President Davis and Secretary of State Toombs felt that the South could achieve independence either by outlasting the North in civil war or by gaining the recognition of foreign powers. They and most other Southerners felt more certain of ultimate international acceptance than of ultimate victory on the battlefield. The South had long known it had a trump card, a card which emboldened many of its political leaders to risk war for it would certainly bring quick foreign aid: cotton.

Cotton began as the Confederacy's greatest asset and became its greatest liability. Its value had been amply proved: in 1860 the Southern States produced 5,400,000 bales, two-thirds of the world total. The textile mills of England, France, the rest of Europe, depended on the South for raw material, and should the supply be cut off by war, unemployment, depression, and untold misery would spread. The Confederate States stood in the happy position of producing a world necessity; the Confederacy's future must concern every nation with large textile interests.

The basis of Confederate diplomacy never changed: cotton served as bait. If Europe wanted it, Europe must come and get it, must keep Confederate ports open, must virtually underwrite Southern independence.

Rebel diplomacy may be divided into three phases: 1) confidence, 2) disillusion, 3) desperation.

Belligerent Rights. Marked by optimism and demanding truculence, the first phase represented the heyday of King Cotton. It marked, too, the acme of Southern inexperience and naïveté. Robert Toombs, abetted by Jefferson Davis, first tried a simple deal. In April, 1861, he sent an ill-chosen threesome—William L. Yancey, Pierre A. Rost, A. Dudley Mann—to offer England and France cotton in exchange for recognition. Shortly after these men arrived in London, Britain and France proclaimed their neutrality in the Civil War, but granted Belligerent Rights to the Confederacy. This boon—and boon it was for it gave Confederate ships and soldiers international equality with their enemies—came without Southern pressure. And since belligerency ranked barely a step from full recognition of independence, the Confederate commissioners felt elated. One interview with British officials should do the trick.

The first interview with Lord John Russell, British Foreign Secretary, set the pattern for future meetings; Russell was courteous, listened well, but kept the meeting unofficial and non-committal. Yancey, Rost, and Mann acted in good and gullible faith; they played their trump card at once. Why not? The logic of King Cotton was irrefutable—duplicity had no place in straightforward business dealings. Russell heard them out, asked sharp questions about Southern resources, determination, and the problem of the slave trade. Apparently satisfied with the answers, he assured the Confederate agents that Her Majesty's Cabinet soon would discuss Southern independence. Much apparently depended on France. Most encouraging, thought the commissioners.

Early French Attitude. Judge Rost journeyed to Paris for a talk with Napoleon III. He missed seeing the Emperor, but discussed Confederate fortunes with Count Charles Louis de Morny, Napoleon III's half-brother and confidant. De Morny, too, offered encouragement. France, he said, sympathized with the Confederacy and certainly desired a weakened American Union. But France must act in concert with Britain. If Victoria proposed recognition, Napoleon would join her. This "Alphonse-Gaston" impasse between England and France plagued Southern diplomacy throughout the war.

Question of Timing. Had King Cotton failed? The commissioners thought not; the problem hinged on bad timing. Textile mills in England and France had comfortable surpluses of cotton on hand. The 1860 crop bulged warehouses, and opulence permitted diplomatic caution. A Confederate victory in the field would do as well as a cotton shortage, reported the commissioners, and promised to demand formal recognition as soon as they learned of a favorable battle. In early August they heard from Robert M. T. Hunter, new Secretary of State, that the Confederate Army under General P. G. T. Beauregard had won a brilliant decision over the Union forces at Manassas, Virginia, on July 21, 1861. The time had come for formal approaches. But again Russell proved aloof; he refused, in fact, to see the Confederates and asked for their news in writing. After he read their communication, he promised further consideration.

Legality of Blockade This surprising coolness abroad forced President Davis to another approach suggested by his legal mind. He knew that according to international agreement, a blockade must be effective to be legal. If Europe would not rush to recognition, it might be willing to concede the illegality of Lincoln's blockade—and unhindered commerce promised victory as surely as foreign acknowledgment. Through the Secretary of State and in public messages to Congress, Davis hammered the theme of a "paper blockade." Lincoln's cordon, he repeated, leaked like a sieve, hence had no claim to international acceptance. Doubtless a good and valid point, but again England and France took note of the argument and ignored it. Davis and the Confederacy began to learn hard lessons of diplomacy: right might be right, but irrelevant.

U. S.-British Relations. Luck gave more diplomatic advantages to the South than negotiations. Not only did luck have a large hand in the award of belligerency, but it also played a major role in fomenting a dangerous crisis in relations between England and the United States late in 1861. Despite all the diplomatic advantages in Yankee hands, Secretary of State William H. Seward, a shrewd and deadly minister, always viewed English attitudes toward the South with suspicion. In almost every British act he saw favoritism toward the Confederacy. Granting belligerency seemed to him the height of partisanship, although by that act Europe recognized the existence of a state of war and hence gave a flimsy cloak to the blockade. Relations between Washington and London grew increasingly strained as 1861 passed. Any incident might well touch off war with England—and there were those who thought Seward would welcome it. In fact a few felt that he wanted a foreign war as a magnet to attract the South back to the Union.

Mason and Slidell. An incident came as the result of a turn in Confederate diplomacy. Davis, unhappy about the performance of his first commissioners, cancelled their mission and altered tactics abroad. Rost received assignment to Spain, Mann to Belgium, and Yancey was called home. New men for London and Paris were picked with care. For assignment near the Court of St. James, Davis and Hunter selected James M. Mason, Virginia gentleman of station. Rumors credited him with a certain crudity, but he had charm and some culture; of diplomatic talents he had none. These were reserved to the man designated for the Tuileries—John Slidell. A New Yorker converted to Louisiana and the South, Slidell spoke French fluently; radiated graciousness, charm, wit; conversed with urbanity, and connived with blasé daring. The best negotiator ever sent abroad by the South, Slidell should have had control of all European activities, but he and Mason were partners. And, as it happened, they did their best work before they got to their posts.

The "Trent" Affair. In November, 1861, Mason and Slidell took passage to Europe on the British Royal Mail Steamer *Trent*. Shortly out of American waters a U. S. man-of-war commanded by Captain Charles Wilkes, stopped the *Trent*, removed the Confederate emissaries, and deposited them in a Boston prison. British public opinion boiled and war talk could be heard all around London. Lincoln and Seward had gone too far, Britons said: the Queen would not tolerate such an insult to the British flag. Prime Minister Lord Palmerston took a belligerent line in demanding an American apology, alerted English possessions to the possibility of war, warned the War and Naval Ministries to be ready, and looked for French support. Support came not only from France but also from virtually every European nation. Newspapers in most capitals ran indignant editorials and letters from irate readers. Long pent-up resentment against bullying Yankees overflowed. Probably the good sense of Lincoln and Prince Albert saved the situation. Both wanted to negotiate; Seward at length forwarded an apology and returned Mason and Slidell to British protection. The crisis subsided.

Mason and Slidell naturally tried to capitalize on fame born of misadventure. Lionized by English and French dignitaries, both men sought to show that such an act of piracy typified Northern conduct. But the breath of war had been enough; England accepted the Yankee apology and let the issue drop.

Attitude of English Yeomen. After the *Trent* affair, Confederate fortunes apparently waned in England. Though Palmerston, Russell, and especially Chancellor of the Exchequer William Gladstone were more friendly to the South than they showed, they took no overt action. Pro-Southern agitation in Parliament, where there were numerous champions of the Southern cause, embarrassed the government but did not win wide support. Pro-Union sentiment grew in the textile counties, where a creeping cotton famine brought real hardship. Sturdy English yeomen tightened their belts and supported abolition over bread—and their staunch stand had more to do with the final negation of Southern diplomacy than is usually conceded.

Judah P. Benjamin. In February, 1862, Davis became President of the Confederate States under the Permanent Constitution. He kept most of his cabinet, but in March moved Judah P. Benjamin from the War Office to the State Department. Unfortunately, he did this not because he knew Benjamin to be best qualified for the post, but rather as a means of hitting back at an angry Congress. Benjamin's administration of the War Department had alienated a good many people and had even provoked an offer of resignation from Stonewall Jackson! Ill fortune on the battlefield was laid at Benjamin's door and Congress proposed an embarrassing investigation of his department. Davis named "the brilliant Jew" to be Secretary of State, and gained a facile, shrewd mind for a vital job.

Benjamin made enemies easily, but rarely lost a friend. Portly, bustling, with wispy curls framing a round and restless face, Benjamin had limitless energy. His smiling, almost unctuous eyes hid a calculating perception which accurately assessed men and led them to think him foolish and too affable. Perhaps the brightest member of the cabinet, Benjamin possessed unusual capacity to get along with Davis and enjoyed his full confidence. A cosmopolite, a man of learning, the role of Secretary of State fitted him exactly—maneuver on a world stage challenged all his guile.

Slidell and Napoleon. Benjamin soon learned that Mason thought Confederate chances unfavorable in Great Britain, and that he urged redoubled efforts. While the Administration pondered another wooing of the British, Slidell went to work on Louis Napoleon.

France had many antislavery advocates, some influential ones, but Napoleon's efforts to rejuvenate the glories of the Empire made him occasionally deaf to popular causes. He had interests and whimsies vulnerable to an artful deceiver—and Slidell plied his trade. He found that King Cotton had great appeal to Napoleon. Although the Emperor rose above the masses, he listened with a tender ear to any whisper of economic unrest. Plans for a Mexican venture, plans for stirring the brew of European politics, depended on a healthy French economy, and the economy rested in considerable measure on textiles. Surpluses enjoyed in early 1861 dwindled rapidly, and France felt the pinch of cotton famine.

Napoleon declared his hostility to the Confederate cotton embargo—an unofficial citizens' boycott of production suggested by Davis' administration—but admitted growing unemployment and misery in the mill areas. Slidell offered him a new deal, one authorized by Benjamin: free trade for a specified period and no less than 100,000 bales of cotton in return for recognition. The offer had the backing of the Confederate Senate. (*See Document No. 14.*) By early 1862 it seemed probable that King Cotton would entice France to recognition. Slidell reported confidently to Mason and Davis, but he confessed a certain suspicion of Napoleon. The Emperor had deceived everyone including himself so often he could hardly be counted on for the truth. Exactly what he did about Confederate recognition is hard to determine. The late Frank L. Owsley, perceptive student of the Confederacy and author of *King Cotton Diplomacy,* traced the intricate convolutions of Napoleon's plots and counterplots and indicated that apparently he approached the British several times with suggestions for joint recognition of the South, for dual intervention, or for mediation. The sincerity of the Emperor's assurances that he asked England to join him is open to question. But there can be little doubt that he wanted to end the Civil War short of restoration of the Union. To this purpose he made several recorded efforts.

In early 1862 he presumably authorized the French Ambassador in Washington to visit Richmond on a friendly mission to adjust the position of French consulates in the Confederacy. The Ambassador spied on Davis' government, with Confederate cooperation, and sent Paris a glowing account of Rebel determination and strength. His report, combined with growing need for cotton, led the Emperor in the fall of 1862 to make a move which convinced Slidell and the Richmond authori-

ties that recognition or mediation had come at last:
Napoleon proposed a joint British-French request to
Northern and Southern governments for a six-month
armistice. During the lull ports would be open for cotton
exports, and mediation of the war would be pushed.

Mediation Near. Curiously enough the French suggestion almost coincided with English determination to
insist on mediation. Palmerston, led by Russell and Gladstone, took increasing alarm at the trouble in England's
Midlands. Mills were shutting down, unemployment grew.
And though workers stuck to the Union cause, the Cabinet had to consider national welfare. French plaints of
threatened depression gained sympathetic hearing. Even
before Napoleon mentioned his plan for joint mediation,
Palmerston agreed that the Cabinet must act. And as the
Prime Minister and Foreign Secretary searched for ways
of ending the Civil War, word came of General Robert
E. Lee's brilliant victory at Second Manassas in the last
days of August, and of his invasion of Maryland. Should
he capture an important Northern city or destroy the
Federal army facing him, then the British government
would propose armistice and negotiation. Seward's hardheaded rejection of outside interference surely would
evaporate under the shadow of Confederate cannon.

On October 7, Gladstone made an important speech
in Newcastle in which he lauded the Confederacy, announced that Jefferson Davis had made a nation and an
army, and declared the South had established its right
to independence. Although disavowed by the government,
Gladstone's assertions reflected the unofficial view of
most of the Cabinet. Russell circularized the members in
like terms and placed armistice and mediation on the
agenda. (*See Document No. 15.*)

Now came Napoleon's request for joint action, with
assurance that Spain and Belgium would cooperate. British officials almost agreed, but at the point of decision
learned of the Rebel check at Sharpsburg, Maryland, and
of Lincoln's Emancipation Proclamation. Intervention
must wait for surer knowledge of the South's "future
prospects." Napoleon's request rejected, he did not lose
hope. When word reached him of Lee's brilliant victory
at Fredericksburg in December, he acted by himself and

offered Seward France's good offices in mediating the conflict. Seward, of course, refused the offer.

Early Diplomacy Fails. Confederate diplomats pondered reasons behind European reluctance to aid the South. High on the list of popular causes stood the supposed British and French reliance on American wheat. Seward did threaten a breadstuff embargo if Europe aided the Rebels—and in rasher moments he rattled the fully committed Union saber. The United States would take on all comers, he said, to maintain its territorial integrity. If Palmerston and Napoleon wanted a blood bath, they could have it. There is no doubt that Seward's bombast and the shrewd bullying done by United States diplomats abroad helped curb French and British enthusiasm for recognition. Then, too, Napoleon had other distractions —his energies and fears were bemused by the attempt to put Maximilian and Carlota on the Mexican throne. When Britain renounced any part in this scheme, he had to guard against United States interference. Although the South offered him a free hand below the Rio Grande, this guarantee might be worthless should the war go badly for the Rebels. Greed forced him to temporize.

Benjamin's Tactics Change. With failure of recognition efforts at the end of 1862, Benjamin turned attention to secondary diplomacy. Time, increasing scarcity of cotton, and Confederate military successes, Benjamin knew, would win independence; while he waited for a more propitious moment to badger Europe, he worked to glean every advantage from belligerency and from cotton.

London "Index." Benjamin ordered Henry Hotze, Confederate propagandist extraordinary, to keep the South before Europe's eyes. He threw the full support of the government behind Hotze's newspaper, the London *Index*. A unique venture in Confederate subsidized publishing, the *Index* offered sound journalism mixed with pro-Southern news. Every Southern victory, every Rebel achievement received space, but so did every Southern setback; hence, Britons and Frenchmen trusted the paper. And this trust Benjamin sought to exploit.

Europe provided far more aid and comfort to the Confederacy than most people realized. Belligerency opened British and continental markets to Southern agents, if they had money. Arms and military equipment manufacturers were usually more willing to sell to the South when fortunes seemed bright; the image of the South presented by the *Index* could immeasurably strengthen the South's commercial position. Hotze worked to fashion an attitude of trust, and did a remarkably good job.

Problems of Blockade Running. Benjamin joined with other government officers in procuring supplies and munitions from abroad. As Secretary of War he struggled to obtain all types of equipment from England and Europe; as Secretary of State he helped organize efforts to thwart the Union blockade, export cotton, and import war matériel. Blockade running started late in 1861, when Federal ships began making appearances at major Southern ports. And as the U. S. Navy organized the cordon, blockade runners systematized evasion. The Confederate government, though, stayed out of the business for some time. Davis tried to convince the world that the blockade did not exist; therefore he could not permit the government to engage openly in blockade running. Private business suffered no theoretical restrictions and many firms in Charleston, Wilmington, North Carolina, Savannah, Mobile, and until its fall, New Orleans, realized fantastic profits from the trade. Rumor had it that by late 1862 one successful round trip through the blockade would pay for a runner; all subsequent trips were sheer profit. So obvious and so rewarding an avenue of trade must not go untapped by the military. Benjamin, vigorously aided by General Josiah Gorgas, the able Chief of Ordnance, finally gained permission from President Davis to engage in a sort of clandestine government trade.

Blockade Running Depots. Benjamin hid the business behind the cloak of regular diplomatic activity. Since the Confederacy had many dealings with West Indian and Caribbean islands and with Bermuda, he sent "commercial agents" to these areas as unofficial consuls. Ostensibly on hand to care for Confederate commercial interests and the personal problems of Southern citizens, these men often doubled as blockade agents. A glance at a map will show the outline of blockade running activity. The Confederacy had over 3,000 miles of coastline cut by numerous rivers, tiny inlets, roadsteads, sounds. The

Federals could not hope to seal off every avenue of access to the South, but most tiny harbors were shallow and inaccessible to large freighters. Consequently, the specially designed, light-draft, speedy blockade runners had come into use. They grew in number each month, and kept up a lively trade from Wilmington to St. George's, Bermuda, and from Charleston and Savannah to Nassau and, occasionally, Havana. Bermuda, a scant 400 miles off North Carolina's coast, became a leading entrepôt for Confederate supplies shipped from England. Freighters stopped at Bermuda, deposited cargoes, picked up cotton in exchange, and returned home. Blockade runners skimmed stealthily through blockading squadrons to Bermuda, discharged cotton, and took on mechandise and munitions. Savannah, Mobile, and other Gulf ports also served as blockade bases.

Government Blockade Runners. Confederate military authorities took steps to funnel as much equipment as possible into the South through the blockade. The most urgent necessity was government control of a large cotton supply for use as credit abroad. Next, it was essential that the Ordnance Bureau and other war agencies have complete control of—perhaps own—some efficient blockade runners. Everything at the Confederate end finally was managed by the War Department. Impressed cotton went to harbors on government account, was put aboard runners, and shipped. And at length, the Ordnance and Medical Bureaus purchased several ships of their own. Affairs in the islands and abroad came under Benjamin's general jurisdiction. Running the blockade in the early years of the war had romantic and exciting overtones, but by mid-1863, it was grim and earnest business.

The Erlanger Loan. In March of 1863, Benjamin and Davis induced Congress to accept the offer of a French banking house, Emile Erlanger & Co., to lend the South $15,000,000, the loan to be secured by cotton bonds. The House of Erlanger would have lent more—Slidell's daughter married into the firm—but the conservative Confederate Congress could not chance bequeathing a heavy national debt to posterity! When the loan opened in European financial centers, scores of unknown Southern purchasing agents descended on Mason, who was

nominally in charge of Confederate funds. Everyone
wanted money to pay off a contract, grease a palm, build
a ship. James D. Bulloch, fabulous Confederate Navy
Agent, hoped for Erlanger funds to assist in finishing
ships in Scotland destined for Southern colors. Mason
saw there were too many agents, all working against each
other. He had been working largely through two import-
export firms, S. Isaac, Campbell & Co., and Fraser, Trenholm & Co., in procuring supplies. Both these firms had
been willing to receive Confederate cotton, sell it at the
market price, and credit receipts to Mason. But the agents
from countless government bureaus, from military departments and Southern States all clamored for special
dispensation. In the financial chaos, Mason knew the
government must be cheated; S. Isaac, Campbell had been
found keeping a double set of books on Confederate
accounts. Mason could not tend diplomatic niceties and
handle all Confederate monies, too. In May, 1863, he
received authority to turn over all money matters to
Colin J. McRae, special agent for the Erlanger Loan,
who took charge of most purchasing in Europe.

Reorganization of Foreign Purchasing Operations.
McRae's assignment was part of a general reorganization
generated by the Erlanger Loan. But he soon found his
main job to be sustaining the loan as best he could. Because of confusion, overlapping of effort, and no clear
line of authority abroad, the loan brought in far less
money than expected. Cash receipts probably totalled no
more than $3,000,000, although an additional $3,000,000
in credits may have been realized. Obviously, much needed
to be repaired in England and France. McRae, working
closely with Benjamin, soon recommended a general re-
alignment of all foreign purchasing activities. With this
in mind, Congress created the Bureau of Foreign Supplies
within the War Department to manage all domestic blockade running activities. McRae took charge of everything
abroad, except formal diplomatic negotiations and some
buying in England. Special agents went to the islands to
improve transshipping and payment procedures.

Estimate of Blockade Running. The reorganization
worked extremely well, but came too late to exploit the
full potential of blockade running. Increased pressure by

the Federal Navy, combined with military reverses, forced the government virtually to nationalize blockade running activities early in 1864. (*See Document No. 16.*) The government put much energy in the trade, and despite the vaunted success of blockading squadrons, runners reached the South right up to the end of the war. Benjamin could take pride in the system. Imperfect, sometimes grossly inefficient and expensive, blockade running nonetheless ranks as one of the most successful ventures undertaken by the government. One authority estimates runners breached the cordon no less than 8,250 times. Through it came some 600,000 small arms, 400,000 blankets, over half a million pounds of coffee, 1,900,000 pounds of salt-peter, and in 1863-1864 alone, 1,500,000 pounds of lead. If blockade running did not win the war for the Confederacy, it staved off defeat for at least two years.

Crisis of 1863. The crisis in Confederate affairs came in 1863. In the period May 1-July 4, Rebel fortunes reached both zenith and nadir. On May 3 Lee's victory at Chancellorsville gladdened the Confederacy and brightened Benjamin's hopes for intervention. He urged Mason and Slidell to renew official requests for recognition and they did their best. By now, though, Europe had grown accustomed to the war, had made some adjustment to the cotton shortage, and preferred waiting. Waiting seemed justified when news came of the twin disasters of Gettysburg and Vicksburg suffered during the first week of July. Vicksburg cost the South an entire army and almost 60,000 small arms; Gettysburg cost 20,000 casualties—both together took a terrible toll in Southern morale. After these defeats, Benjamin and Davis had little hope for the success of King Cotton. The illusion of invincibility vanished. Cotton had never been King and now the would-be Kingdom reeled under mortal blows.

Consuls expelled. For a time disillusion gave way to anger and a desire to strike back at an unheeding Europe. Simmering irritation with British consuls came to a head in late 1863. When the consul in Richmond began to arrogate ambassadorial duties to himself, Benjamin expelled all of Her Majesty's representatives. Mason, abandoning hope for English help, left his post for Paris. Congress shared the resentment against foreign hostility, and refused to accredit a commissioner to Russia late in the year.

Mexico. Benjamin knew the South would get no help from England or France without heroic achievement in the field. After 1863 he gave more and more attention to Mexico. The appointment of John T. Pickett, swash-buckler, adventurer, filibusterer, as emissary to Mexico in 1861 had been a serious error. Wild-eyed and unscrupulous, Pickett brandished bribes and permitted his correspondence with Richmond to be regularly intercepted by canny Yankee agents. He languished in a Mexican jail shortly after reaching the country and was no match for the able United States Minister, Thomas Corwin.

If Confederate officials cherished hopes for Maximilian's favor, these faded as the Emperor's troubles with Mexican patriot Benito Juarez increased. Imperial Mexico eroded, and Maximilian relied more heavily on Napoleon. Finally, he pinned his future on United States recognition. With that, of course, any chance for a deal with the Confederacy vanished. But in the North Mexican States an independent governor ran a vast domain with little concern for Maximilian or Juarez. Santiago Vidaurri apparently liked the South, certainly he liked the rich trade which passed from Texas to Matamoras, and responded generously to the blandishments offered by special Confederate agent Juan A. Quintero. Quintero had perhaps more commercial success than any diplomat. Negotiating with Vidaurri, with Maximilian, and with Juarez, he kept open the fabulously bawdy port of Bagdad, near Matamoras, and kept cotton trains moving across the wasteland of South Texas throughout the war. Bagdad-Matamoras probably handled more Confederate freight than any other port.

Canadian Ventures. The reverses of 1864 brought growing desperation. Benjamin thought something might be achieved by a group of secret agents sent to Canada, from whence they could encourage disloyal elements in the North—the Copperheads, Knights of the Golden Circle, Sons of Liberty. Some agents did attempt to free Confederate prisoners in Yankee camps, but these were last-gasp measures and came to nothing.

The Kenner Mission. Davis and Benjamin played

their final hand in February, 1865. They sent reliable and reputable Duncan F. Kenner on a secret mission of the most desperate kind. Sailing from New York in disguise, Kenner went to Paris with a message of grave import for Mason and Slidell: they were to offer emancipation to England and France in exchange for recognition and assistance. Mason could not believe the cause had sunk so low, but returned to England and a last interview with Palmerston on March 14, 1865. The Prime Minister exuded sympathy, but still waited for Confederate victory. Slidell saw Napoleon and asked if slavery stood in the way of recognition, only to be told that the Emperor had never taken the subject into account in thinking about the Civil War. Napoleon reiterated his standard promise: he would move when England did. So, with the cornerstone of the Confederacy put on the block, the South lost its last diplomatic round. A few weeks later General Lee surrendered his army and the Confederacy disintegrated.

Estimate of Diplomacy. On balance King Cotton diplomacy failed. Why? Did Southern statesmen fail, did their policies fail, or were they victims of hopeless circumstance? All of these factors combined to wreck Rebel hopes abroad. Confederate statesmen aimed at a false objective in recognition. Recognition alone would not have won the war for the South. Attempts to have the blockade declared invalid were more realistic, but not sternly pushed. The King Cotton mania, which denied all other avenues of pressure, proved too brittle a policy and when it failed, Confederates had no alternatives. But had objectives been sound and policies adroit, would independence have been secured abroad? Probably not, for a tide of liberalism ran in the nineteenth century and slavery could not stand against it. Confederate statesmen finally recognized the abiding affection for freedom cherished in Europe, but offered abolition for independence too late.

Britain held the key to Confederate diplomacy throughout the war—if Britain moved, France and others were pledged to follow. All efforts to stimulate British activity proved futile; in retrospect the reasons are clear. Despite a certain romantic attachment among the nobility to a Cavalier crusade, stolid English yeomen were willing to go hungry in support of freedom. And perhaps of equal importance, British military forces were hopelessly decayed; Palmerston dared not risk war with the United States unless Confederate armies took up most Yankee energies. Weak British efforts might cost Canada.

The best Southern chance rested always with Confederate soldiers. When they gained victories, independence came close; when they lost, nothing else mattered.

— 5 —

"THAT INCOMPARABLE INFANTRY"

Confederate soldiers, fond of a good song and especially of one with a sound moral, collected a group of biblical paraphrases into a marching ditty which they called the "Texas Bible"—probably because Texas troops started the collecting. One of the verses went like this:

The race is not to them that's got, the longest legs to run,
Nor the battle to the people that shoots the biggest gun.

And pretty much the whole history of the Confederate soldier can be summed up by saying that he tried to prove what he sang.

Qualities of Confederate Soldiers. At the start it looked to the Confederates as though they had an equal, or better than equal chance. But time, attrition, desertion, and decay behind the lines changed the picture, and in the last months only the hardiest veterans still marched with Lee and Joe Johnston. But those few typified Rebel soldiers; the deeds they did became a splendid part of the American military tradition. When in the end they were beaten, they were soundly beaten; but they had been hard to beat. The reasons for their long and remarkable effort are many. They were a special breed; they had exceptional leaders; they believed in their cause; they fought to defend their homes; they waged a war which to some extent gave them advantage of geographic position; they refused to accept defeat until most of them were gone and they had nothing left to fight with.

Who were the Southern soldiers? They came from all parts of the South and every station in life. Elite units flourished for a time, and boasted esoteric philosophers and Latin-reading privates. Even conscript units, prevalent after the draft laws of 1862, often sported their quota of poetry fanciers, along with back country bumpkins who contributed their share of Elizabethan vulgarisms and bawdy stories. They were strong men, weak men, fierce men, lewd men, saintly men, confused, frightened, timid, gentle men. Like their Yankee brethren, they were Americans from everywhere banded together for a cause. And they had another bond, one that set them apart from all other American soldiers—a peculiar, almost indescribable *esprit*. All armies, if they are any good, develop an *esprit*, but the South's armies were unique in theirs. It transcended the dirt, the dying, the dearth, and the final dreary hopelessness. It transcended staggering losses, grinding attrition, bad generals. It transcended, even, the Confederacy. The only explanation is that it was the result of a special sort of comradeship—a comradeship which produced the Army of Northern Virginia and the Army of Tennessee. One of their enemies labeled these armies for history: "That incomparable infantry."

Confederate Military Leaders. Leadership had much to do with forging the mettle of the Confederate armies. Tradition has it that most of the talented officers of the United States Army and Navy in the ante bellum decades were Southerners and that they resigned their commissions to join the Confederacy. Many did resign or emerge from civilian life to accept Confederate commissions, but not as many as legend allows. Still the list is impressive. To name a few army men: Pierre Gustave Toutant Beauregard, irrepressible Creole; J. E. B. Stuart, of jingling spurs, flourishing beard and Cavalier manner; Joseph E. Johnston, Virginia gentleman and oft-wounded soldier-engineer; Thomas Jonathan Jackson, dour professor at Virginia Military Institute, latent genius; James Longstreet, Georgian, gruff and dogged; Albert Sidney Johnston, Kentucky wonder, most experienced of Old Army men, veteran of Texas fighting, leader of the ill-starred Utah Expedition, friend of Jefferson Davis; Braxton Bragg, North Carolinian, another friend of Davis, methodical, dedicated, too meticulous; Nathan Bedford Forrest, Tennessee trooper, self-taught soldier extraordinary;

Gideon J. Pillow, another Tennessean, politician, Mexican War misadventurer, military incompetent; and Robert Edward Lee, Virginian.

Navy men included Josiah Tattnall, Franklin Buchanan, Isaac Newton Brown, John Newland Maffitt, and Raphael Semmes of the *Alabama*.

N. B. Forrest. In such a coterie there were bound to be prima donnas, political hacks, mediocrities, and great soldiers. President Davis had to deal with all types and attempt to winnow the good from the bad. War, of course, did much of the winnowing, and in balance, there were more competent than incompetent gray captains. From so many it is difficult to pick the best, but three deserve special mention. Forrest was a natural leader, an intrepid cavalryman who dazzled his compatriots and baffled his foes, a hero of the West whose action at Brice's Cross Roads, Mississippi, June 10, 1864, became a model of cavalry tactics.

Stonewall Jackson. Solemn faced, bewhiskered T. J. Jackson, V. M. I. professor of Artillery Tactics, probably the most remarkable man produced by Confederate martial alchemy, had spent a long and moderately obscure career in the U. S. Army. Distinction in the Mexican War had later been marred by personal acerbity and health faddism. By 1861 Jackson ranked as the most unpopular teacher at V. M. I, as a sort of Presbyterian fanatic, a "crackpot." His inner warmth and affection were glimpsed by few, but one cadet pierced the cold exterior to see Jackson as a "grand, gloomy and peculiarly *good* man." On the battlefield, Jackson changed completely, became a hard-driving, relentless leader who pushed his men to the utmost and won victory after victory. (*See Document No. 17.*) After he and his disciplined brigade held the embattled Confederate left flank at First Manassas in July, 1861, Jackson was known to history as "Stonewall." It is a poor nickname in view of his hallmarks: swift marching, careful scouting, fierce attack, and tireless pursuit. But the name stuck, and helped mold the Confederate spirit. A peerless leader in battle, a splendid example of practicing Christian, Jackson gave his own troops a spark that made them mighty.

Robert E. Lee. But Robert E. Lee comes from history as the greatest of Confederates. Stately, erect, his finely-shaped face framed by white hair and beard, Lee had steady and kind eyes. His graceful carriage, patrician appearance, compassionate nature might seem at first glance out of place in military garb, but a close look reveals the firmness and audacity of a great general. History called Lee to be more than a general—he became a symbol, the soul of an army, a nation's hope, the embodiment of a cause. And when the cause vanished, a broken people looked to him as the symbol of a New South. Lee met all these requirements, and is, hence, remembered not only as a great soldier but also as a great man.

Art of War in 1861. Like all Civil War commanders, Lee started the war with limited military vision. The art of war by 1861 had been conditioned by the thinking of Henri Jomini and Napoleon Bonaparte. American officers learned the campaigns and military theories of these "greats" in sketchy history courses at the U. S. Military Academy, but spent more time on engineering. Limited military theory had been supplemented for many young officers by experience in the Mexican War, but in 1861 prevailing concepts of war dictated small armies operating in isolation, with some attention given to Jomini's doctrine of the defensive-offensive, and much concern lavished on defense of fortified positions.

The fell hand of Sir Walter Scott had something to do with the state of Southern military thinking. Clausewitz, in his classic treatise *On War,* preached the virtues of total combat, but Jomini gave gentlemanly language to hard military lessons and permitted Southerners to construe war in Scottian terms. The result: gentlemen against gentlemen, with civilians remaining excluded innocents.

The North shared the non-combatant idea of civilians, and to some extent the gentlemanly view of conflict. Both sides were utterly unprepared for the magnitude of the war which began in 1861. Old ideas of army size, of army supply, and especially of army command, broke down in the Civil War. Northern and Southern generals and civilian leaders had to alter old views, had to change completely the management of armies, societies, and economies to meet the stresses of modern combat. The Civil

War deserves the designation of "first of the modern wars," not only because it saw the first military use of the railroad, of the submarine, of the machine gun, of the ironclad railroad gun, of chemical warfare, of a rudimentary air service, but also because of the changes in ground combat tactics involving infantry, artillery, and cavalry.

Confederate Strategy. Jefferson Davis is often condemned by historians for failing to devise a national strategy for the South. He is criticized for sticking to a defensive plan which forced him to hold many Confederate troops in static coastal and interior positions. The charge is leveled that defensive war is essentially sterile, robs a nation of military vigor, and dooms its armies to receiving attack where the enemy wills. Especially, assert critics, is it fatal for an inferior power to await the pleasure of a much stronger enemy. And Davis, by adopting defense, sapped Confederate strength and withheld vital troops from the field. These charges are based on a misinterpretation of Davis' strategic ideas. He did evolve a national strategy for the Confederacy, one which comported well with known military theory and with Confederate strengths and weaknesses. Its defensive features were more apparent than real. The Confederate President had always to wage war within a state rights framework; his desire to abandon Southern sod in order to concentrate men for offensive operations had always to yield to the alarms and fears of such governors as Brown and Vance.

And there is a possibility that military concentration—the ideal of Jomini and the constant charm of Joseph E. Johnston and other generals—had less merit than textbooks claimed. It is easy to argue, as many did, that the best defense is a good offense; that the South should yield its ports, its precious acres, concentrate its legions, and strike a decisive blow; that victory would redeem lost ground. True, if victory is the goal. But Davis clearly understood the Confederacy did not need to win the war; like the American colonies in the earlier Revolution, the South needed merely to avoid losing. It wanted only to be left alone, to repulse invasion. While Davis always believed in the offensive for military ends, he believed the

offensive-defensive to be the best politico-military strategy
for the Confederacy.

He stuck to his strategy with remarkable dedication,
modified it with new command ideas, and improved on it
as he could. And with his strategy in mind, a good deal
about the South's war comes clear.

Theaters of War. Basically, the fighting took place
in three sectors, or theaters: the eastern theater, extending as far west as Middle Tennessee and part of Georgia,
Alabama, and Mississippi; the central theater (often
called the "west" in Civil War literature), extending to
the Mississippi River; and the Trans-Mississippi theater,
including Texas, Indian Territory (where the Five Civilized Tribes and some not so civilized became Confederate treaty allies), Arkansas, and occasionally part of
Missouri. (*See Document No. 18.*) Union strategy centered on splitting the Confederacy roughly along these
geographical lines, then chopping up the pieces.

Strategic Importance of Richmond. The most serious
threats to the heart of the South always came in Virginia,
and most Civil War study has centered on that area. But
Virginia is part of the total picture; what happened there
affected the whole war; what happened in other areas affected Virginia.

The Confederate Congress, in a move to confirm affection for Virginia, voted to move the capital from
Montgomery to Richmond in May, 1861. Richmond had
some advantages: in it were the vital Tredegar Iron Works
and perhaps the most important cluster of manufacturing
plants in the South; it symbolized the Old Dominion and
as the Confederate capital would add to the strength of
the government. And with the South's principal city so far
north, some border areas might be induced to join the
cause. But Richmond's great disadvantage was that it
rested a scant hundred miles from Washington and would
be a constant military objective. There is much to be said
for the argument that the capital should never have been
moved so close to Yankeeland, for it remained a deadly
magnet to Federal efforts. Northern strategy remained
relatively consistent: press all the frontiers of the Confederacy to embattle every Rebel soldier and prevent
concentration, and at the same time exert direct pressure

on Richmond. "On to Richmond" was the Yankee battle-cry for four years—the idea behind it being that the whole Rebel structure would fall with the capital.

First Manassas. In keeping with a peaceful posture, the Confederates made no aggressive moves. Instead, they concentrated on mustering and organizing their armies and waited to see what the Federals did. Federal preparations were as slow as those of the South, but given the chance to attack first, the North made the most of it. In July, 1861, a large Union army under General Irvin McDowell started for Richmond but came to grief in the Battle of First Manassas (Bull Run in Yankee parlance), July 21. The battle proved a costly victory for the South. It convinced many Confederates that the war had all but ended and that Rebel armies were invincible. On the other hand, it convinced the North that the war had just begun and that the Rebellion had more strength than anticipated.

Late 1861 and Early 1862. Small encounters took place in various parts of the South during the remainder of 1861, but neither side felt ready for a major effort. Not until early 1862 did war resume in earnest. Then it blazed in the far west with an ill-fated Confederate offensive into New Mexico in February and March, and erupted at the same time in the Mississippi Basin. In the central theater the Yankees moved first, this time with a combined expedition of land and naval forces aimed at the Tennessee and Cumberland Rivers—both of which offered natural invasion routes to the heart of the Deep South. Short, stubble-whiskered, cigar-chewing, methodical, General Ulysses S. Grant commanded the Union effort. Against him stood General Albert Sidney Johnston, who had his troubles from the beginning. Charged with defending the middle of the Confederacy's northern frontier, Johnston had too few men and almost no artillery or powder. By cagy bluffing and commendable bravado, his men stuck in southern Kentucky and held on to Tennessee. The keys to the entire Confederate front, however, were Fort Henry on the Tennessee and Fort Donelson on the Cumberland. They had to be held. Grant's amphibious tactics took both forts by mid-February 1862, and the gateway to the South swung wide.

Shiloh. Grant pressed ahead and in April had established a land base near Shiloh Church in Tennessee. From this base he expected to move against Johnston's main positions at Corinth, Mississippi. But now the Confederates were ready to strike back, to apply the principles of the offensive-defensive. Johnston called for help from across the Mississippi, where General Earl Van Dorn commanded a small Southern army, and made ready to attack Grant. Unfortunately for Johnston, Van Dorn had suffered defeat at Elkhorn Tavern, Arkansas, March 6-8, and consequently could offer help to no one.

Unaware of Van Dorn's misfortune, Johnston moved from Corinth toward Shiloh and on April 6 gained a complete surprise over Grant's army. A signal Confederate victory seemed certain, but Albert Sidney Johnston sustained a mortal wound during the day and command passed to General Beauregard, recently come from Virginia. Beauregard did his best to continue the victory, but nightfall halted the battle. During the night, reinforcements came to Grant and the next day Beauregard found retreat the better part of valor. The Battle of Shiloh, however, had lasting strategic importance for the Confederacy. It tarnished Grant's star and brought lethargic General Henry W. Halleck to the west. The main result was that it solidified the Confederate front in the central theater for almost a year. Although the South lost Tennessee and found its middle border shoved back to northern Mississippi, Shiloh stopped further enemy penetration; hence, although a tactical defeat, it deserves recognition as a limited strategic success.

McClellan Prepares. After the tragic loss of New Orleans to Admiral David G. Farragut late in April—a nearly mortal blow—Confederate attention shifted again to Virginia, where a new Yankee general prepared an expedition against Richmond. General George B. McClellan had come from some successes in western Virginia to whip the Army of the Potomac into shape and lead it to victory. McClellan is a curious figure in the war; brilliant, cocky, capable of winning the deathless devotion of his men, he had a lurking character flaw which immobilized him at the moment of attack. He could organize and drill a magnificent army—did, in fact, make the Army of the

Potomac the best in the North—but could not commit it when the time came. As Lincoln perceptively put it, McClellan "had the slows." But he worked like a demon and decided, as Grant had done, to use the naval superiority of the Union to move his army by water to Chesapeake Bay, base himself at Yorktown on the Peninsula between the York and James rivers, and advance on Richmond from its exposed southeastern flank.

Seven Pines. Yankee preparations were closely watched by Southern spies in Washington and by Confederate cavalry pickets; McClellan's intentions to move were known to General Joseph E. Johnston, now in command of the Rebel army still concentrated near Manassas Junction. When McClellan's men were almost ready, Johnston destroyed vast supply depots at Manassas and retired to the Peninula. Shrewd guessing enabled him to meet McClellan almost as soon as the Federals landed. Lack of naval strength made Confederate flanks vulnerable, and Johnston backed slowly up the Peninsula, lending currency to a new nickname—"Retreatin' Joe Johnston." But Old Joe had his moment. At Seven Pines, a few miles from Richmond, he surprised McClellan's hordes on May 31, 1862. Johnston received a severe wound during the battle, but his men gained some success. Had he been able to continue in command his plan to roll up the Union left flank might have succeeded, but in his absence the fruits of victory slipped from Confederate grasp.

Lee in Command. At this critical point, Davis called on General Lee to take charge of Johnston's force, now designated the Army of Northern Virginia. Lee accepted, and began immediately to plot ways of defeating McClellan. For the moment, McClellan appeared content with digging elaborate trenches and inching forward by "regular approaches." Lee used the time to call for reinforcements.

Jackson's Valley Campaign. His eye fell at once on the small Confederate army of about 18,000 men under Stonewall Jackson in the Shenandoah Valley. The Army of the Valley, by the beginning of June, 1862, had earned considerable reputation. Jackson, in one of the finest examples of the offensive-defensive, had hurled his little

band against four Federal armies, attacked each sepa-
rately, defeated them in succession, and pinned no less
than 60,000 bluecoats in the grain-rich Shenandoah—
bluecoats who should have been helping McClellan attack
Richmond. Jackson fought several battles, many combats,
and countless skirmishes; marched his men almost beyond
endurance; and made the "foot cavalry" the hardest hitting force in the war. So thoroughly did he do his job of
holding the Valley and detaining the enemy, that Lee
considered the Shenandoah safe enough to call the Valley
Army to Richmond to assist in attacking the Army of
the Potomac.

Seven Days' Battles and Cedar Mountain. On June
26, Lee, aided by Jackson's army, launched the Seven
Days' Battles, which lasted through July 1. Confederate
troops hurled the Union Army back from its lines four
miles from Richmond to a small beachhead on the James
River, where the Yankees cowered under cover of gunboats. These brilliant battles lifted the siege of Richmond,
and brought an opportunity for a sustained Confederate
offensive. With Davis' full approval, Lee applied once
again offensive-defensive strategy. He detached Jackson
with a corps of the army to strike another Union force
moving into northern Virginia over the old route from
Washington. Part of this new enemy force, commanded by
hapless General John Pope, Jackson met and routed at
Cedar Mountain on August 9. Lee joined Jackson with the
rest of the army and pursued Pope relentlessly.

Second Manassas. General Lee came increasingly
to trust Jackson for any independent assignment, and
soon asked him to take his corps on a wide sweep around
Pope's right flank, hit enemy communications, destroy
supplies, and force an enemy concentration against him.
The foot cavalry marched rapidly on Manassas Junction,
wrecked a huge Union supply base, and Jackson made
ready to meet Pope near the battlefield of First Manassas.
On August 29-30 Jackson's men beat off determined blue
attacks in the Battle of Second Manassas; Lee brought up
the other corps of his army, commanded by General
James Longstreet, and joined Jackson's men in a splendid
victory which ran the Federals once again across Bull
Run.

Davis' General Offensive. By now President Davis had hatched a new plan. While Lee's men did great deeds in Virginia, Davis learned that Braxton Bragg was almost ready to carry the war back into Tennessee and hoped, perhaps, to redeem Kentucky. Davis decided on a huge, concerted Confederate drive into the enemy's country—the best single application of the offensive-defensive strategy. Suggesting to General Edmund Kirby Smith in East Tennessee that he cooperate with Bragg, Davis wrote Smith, Lee, and Bragg that they would take Southern banners to the North, not as conquerers, but as liberators and peacemakers. He wanted the world to see Confederate strength and note at the same time Confederate forbearance. (*See Document No. 19.*)

Bragg's Kentucky Expedition. Bragg's Kentucky expedition has been maligned by historians as an example of the general's innate inability to do anything other than plan and organize. Like McClellan, Bragg appeared to lack nerve at crucial moments. After outmaneuvering Union forces under General Don Carlos Buell, Bragg reached the vicinity of Louisville, a large Federal base. Instead of attacking the city or threatening Buell's army, he sidled off to Frankfort, Kentucky, to install a Confederate governor in a puppet chair. His nerve failed him, say historians; he missed his greatest chance and may well have lost the war. This judgment appears too harsh in light of recent studies. Bragg suffered under a peculiar command arrangement which Davis originated. The President, in a sound attempt to delegate some military responsibility, established a geographical department system, with a general in charge of each department and all the forces in it. These department commanders were often too autonomous; Kirby Smith was one of them, and he certainly retained far more latitude of decision than an officer subordinate to Bragg should have had. Since Smith commanded a separate geographical area and a separate army, Bragg could not order his cooperation in the invasion; instead he had to suggest and request. Smith obeyed and disobeyed as he pleased. Hence, the final failure of the campaign—and failure it was, for Bragg retreated from Kentucky—rests heavily on Smith. In the two pitched battles which Bragg fought during the campaign, though, Perryville (October 8) and Murfrees-boro (December 31-January 2, 1863), he deserves blame for tactical incapacity.

Lee Invades Maryland. Lee did his best to carry out Davis' strategic ideas in concert with Bragg. Bragg's columns marched from Chattanooga on the first stage of the Kentucky campaign two days before Jackson's men met Pope at Second Manassas. As soon as it was clear that Pope had been beaten, Lee faced a serious decision: should he refit and regroup or invade Maryland? His men had been fighting for two solid months, marching and skirmishing almost every day. They were tired, worn, their supplies thin, transportation rickety, ammunition low. At the same time, the only way to take part in Davis' general offensive would be to invade Maryland. On September 5, Lee's men crossed the Potomac for the first time; Confederate banners were near the heart of the Union! But exultation was short-lived. McClellan, called back to command Pope's shattered legions, followed Lee westward and engaged segments of the Confederate army near Sharpsburg on September 16. Lee had detached Stonewall on another lone venture to capture the Union base at Harpers Ferry. Jackson took the base and marched swiftly to aid the commanding general at Sharpsburg. On September 17 his men stood like a stone wall on the Confederate left and may well have saved the army of Northern Virginia from utter ruin. Sharpsburg (Antietam) was the most fearsome battle the war had yet known; hour by hour it hung in desperate balance and ended in a cruel sort of draw. Lee contemplated attacking McClellan on the 18th, but neither army could renew such slaughter. On the 19th Lee crossed the Potomac to Virginia, leaving 10,000 casualties behind.

Davis' New Command System. So Davis' great offensive failed. In wake of Sharpsburg, Lincoln issued his Preliminary Emancipation Proclamation, and this may have had more to do with later events than the blunting of the Rebel drives in the center and east. But Davis refused to be daunted. He did seek, however, to improve on obvious deficiencies in his command structure. In late 1862, despite extreme dislike for the man, he asked a mended Joe Johnston to take the greatest command ever offered to a Confederate general. To supplant his former departmental system, Davis gave Johnston a theater command, the Department of the West, embracing a vast domain from the western edges of North Carolina and Georgia to the Mississippi and extending as far north as Johnston could exercise control. In addition, he had over-all supervision of the armies already in his satrapy.

As things worked out, Johnston did not make full use of his powers, partly because of certain innate qualms and partly because Davis never made clear the authority conferred on the Department Commander. Johnston found it virtually impossible to give direct orders to Bragg's Army of Tennessee, or demand coordination between Bragg and General John C. Pemberton, charged with defending the Confederacy's vital bastion at Vicksburg on the Mississippi. Davis apparently hoped that Johnston would coordinate all military and logistical operations in his area and thus secure both the northern frontier and Vicksburg.

Vicksburg Campaign. But when Grant renewed his campaign to seize the Mississippi River in mid-1863, Johnston did no more than order a few reinforcements from Bragg to Pemberton. Grant, after an initial check at Holly Springs, Mississippi, again took to the water and moved a huge expedition against Vicksburg's river flank. At length he succeeded in passing the city's formidable batteries and landed below Pemberton's defenses. Pemberton, caught without cavalry and with conflicting orders from Davis and Johnston, finally retired into his imposing fortifications to endure a siege which began in mid-May. On July 4, 1863, he surrendered the city, some 30,000 men, and invaluable ordnance supplies to Grant. The Confederacy was at last cut in twain and began a precarious dual existence.

The Trans-Mississippi Department at length became an almost independent segment of the South. General E. Kirby Smith took command west of the River, and exercised such autonomy that the entire Western Confederacy gained the nickname "Kirby-Smithdom."

Chancellorsville. While the drama on the Mississippi progressed, Lee had been more than holding his own in

Virginia. Although forced to retire after Sharpsburg, the Army of Northern Virginia smashed a foolish assault by the Army of the Potomac under General Ambrose Burnside at Fredericksburg in December, 1862, and Lee's men spent the winter around that lovely town recruiting and refitting. With spring, a new Yankee leader, General Joseph Hooker, undertook to do what his predecessors had not done: flank and finish Lee. On May 1 and 2, Lee's columns left their Fredericksburg lines, marched westward into the Wilderness country, and met Hooker near Chancellorsville. On May 2, Stonewall Jackson received and carried out his greatest orders: flank the Union right, hit Hooker from the rear. Beginning at daylight, Jackson's corps marched fifteen miles to the enemy's rear and a little after five in the afternoon, unleashed the most devastating attack yet mounted by Lee's army. Hooker's broken units fled; demoralized men and animals raced over the battlefield; Hooker's headquarters came under shellfire. Ruin—utter, complete, and humiliating—faced the Army of the Potomac. Only nightfall; and the tragic wounding of Jackson—his own men shot him by mistake on a dark back road—saved Hooker. As it was, he lost the battle, crossed the Rappahannock River, and retired from army command.

Gettysburg. Chancellorsville stands as the costliest of Confederate victories—Jackson died of his wounds on May 10. At the same time, it offered another opportunity for Lee to carry the war to the enemy and to ease pressure on the west. He determined on a move north into Pennsylvania to draw Yankee reinforcements, to collect supplies and, perhaps, to gain foreign recognition for the South. At Gettysburg, July 1-3, 1863, his northern venture ended.

Gettysburg—battle of epic proportions, of masses on opposing hills, of serried lines of flashing guns and blazing muskets, of commonplace heroism, of terrible slaughter, and of Pickett's Charge—cost Lee at least 20,000 casualties and forced his return to Virginia. It was a battle Lee probably should not have fought; his new command arrangements, made in wake of Jackson, failed and the army fought in bits and pieces instead of in concert.

First Week of July 1863. Many historians argue

that Gettysburg marks the turning point in the war, that it deserves to be known as the decisive battle. Others, and these are in growing number, maintain that losses in the west, particularly at Vicksburg, were more important to the final outcome. There is merit to both arguments; Gettysburg has the drama, Vicksburg the strategic importance. It is safe to say that the first week of July, 1863, was decisive—it produced a crisis Davis' administration never overcame. Fifty thousand Confederate soldiers were killed, wounded, or captured that week, and 70,000 small arms lost or given up. These were mortal losses, for men and weapons were irreplaceable.

Chickamauga and Missionary Ridge. Faced with this terrible week, Davis clung grimly to his strategy and to Lee. Johnston sank lower yet in the President's esteem, and finally went on the shelf. The Army of Tennessee, still in Bragg's hands, was called on for an offensive late in the year. A major Southern victory might offset some of the gloom arising from the twin July disasters. Bragg did his best, received Longstreet's corps from Lee as reinforcement, and hit General William S. Rosecrans' army at Chickamauga, Georgia, on September 19 and 20. Bragg ran true to form. He gained a smashing victory, drove Rosecrans' men back into Chattanooga, but failed to press the attack. Instead, he established a mincing sort of siege which harassed rather than hindered. In the end he saw his own army beaten in the Battle of Missionary Ridge, November 23-25, 1863. This battle, the height of ineptitude, cost Bragg his command.

Joe Johnston Returns. Out of retirement once more came Joe Johnston. Davis had lost none of his distrust for the acid little general, but yielded to pressure in and out of Congress to reinstate him as commander of the Army of Tennessee. Davis knew all too well that the hopes of the country rested on Lee and Johnston. Kirby Smith, beyond the Mississippi, could get no troops across the river. What happened to the Southern cause depended on the main field armies east of the river. Lee must hold Richmond and Virginia, while Johnston built strength for a drive into Tennessee. Reasons for a Tennessee move were sound—given Confederate knowledge and belief. Davis and his advisers always thought that thousands of men would flock to the cause in Tennessee and Kentucky if given an opportunity. They had failed to come when Bragg gave them a chance in 1862, but the hope lingered. Then, too, a shift of the war northward would provide better food and forage—an increasingly vital consideration.

Preparations for Summer, 1864. Preparations for an advance involved Johnston in vexing problems of supply, transport, and manpower. He had too few men, horses, wagons, shoes, arms, for an offensive. Richmond seemed unsympathetic to an army's housekeeping needs. The President and Secretary of War urged a quick attack, but Johnston took time for caution, for he understood fully the odds General William T. Sherman was building against him. Lee could offer no help; he needed more than he had to meet the huge army General George G. Meade, hero of Gettysburg, was readying for a drive on Richmond.

Grant dictated the strategy for 1864. He became general-in-chief of all Union armies in March, and determined to press the South at all points. His plan for the year involved extensive naval harassment of Southern coasts, an invasion of Smith's domain beyond the River, and coordinated attacks by Meade's and Sherman's armies. If Lee and Johnston both were under pressure, they could hardly help each other. The Union's crusher offensive began in early May, with the Army of the Potomac hitting Lee in the Wilderness and Sherman's 80,-000 striking at Johnston's 45,000 near Dalton, Georgia.

The Richmond Campaign. Lee and Johnston did equally well, and in retrospect both worked wonders of defense. Grant kept Meade's men hammering in the Wilderness. The butcher's bill for Payne's Farm, Spotsylvania, the blood bath at Cold Harbor in early June, was almost more than the North could pay. Finally, Grant took the army across the James and Appomattox Rivers to hit at Petersburg and move on Richmond from behind. At Petersburg, in mid-June, the Army of the Potomac began a siege which was to last nine grueling months. When the siege began, the Yankee campaign had failed, for Lee still held Richmond with an intact army resting on its own base.

The Atlanta Campaign. Sherman seemed more likely to succeed, since Johnston was more outnumbered than Lee. But Sherman ran into serious trouble. Johnston did not like the sobriquet "Retreatin' Joe," but in Georgia that summer he lived up to and beyond it. Displaying rare skill in retreat, he baffled several attempts to catch him, fended off probing Union units, retired in good order inflicting more losses than he sustained, won a significant victory at the Battle of Kenesaw Mountain in June, and fell back on Atlanta. When Sherman formally began the siege of Atlanta in July, he, like Grant, faced an intact Confederate army resting on its base. And like Grant, too, he still had his campaign to win. Davis helped him. Johnston's constant retreating without explaining why to the Chief Executive had strained relations to the limit, and on July 18 Davis replaced him with General John B. Hood. Hood of the sad face, haunted eyes, and maimed body, was widely admired as a hard fighter, but lightly regarded as a military administrator or strategist. He fought well enough. Two vicious attacks from his Atlanta lines cost thousands of precious lives and failed to dislodge Sherman. On September 2, 1864, Hood gave up Atlanta and retreated a safe distance to refit and plan strategy.

Hood's Tennessee Campaign. Davis, too, planned strategy. He returned to his old theater command idea. This time too a presidential opponent got the job. General Beauregard was called from lesser duties to take over what was left of the Department of the West, now slipped considerably eastward. And again Davis did not clearly spell out the Department Commander's responsibilities, with the result that Hood dealt directly with the President and Beauregard became a sort of glorified quartermaster. He confined himself to finding supplies for a new expedition Hood decided to launch into Tennessee. Hood's idea had merit. A quick stike to Tennessee could conceivably draw Sherman back to protect his rear, and would certainly have logistical advantages. The plan hinged on speed, but Hood dawdled along in north Georgia, apparently hoping Sherman would follow and attack on favorable Rebel ground. Sherman instead turned his back on Hood and marched toward the sea. Hood moved into

Tennessee. But by the time he moved in mid-November, everyone knew he was coming. A brief moment of victory was his at Franklin on November 30, but was offset by the total wreckage of his army at Nashville on December 15. The Army of Tennessee virtually disappeared for weeks and when it reassembled under Joe Johnston, only the hardest men were left. Divisions were shattered; brigades reduced to company size. The proud legions of 1862 were gone; a ghost army trudged with Old Joe Johnston to the honor of the end.

Siege of Petersburg. Lee fared better, but the outcome could hardly be in doubt. Trapped in a thirty-mile labyrinth of trenches at Petersburg—a system of ditches similar in size and depth to those on the Western Front in the First World War—Lee had no freedom of maneuver. The Army of Northern Virginia began the siege with about 75,000 men, but daily attrition steadily cut the ranks. Grant kept pouring men into Meade's lines, and the disparity in the size of the armies grew more obvious each day. Faced with the drain of trench attrition and with ranging Union units cutting into various parts of Virginia, including his granary in the Shenandoah, Lee turned again to the offensive-defensive. He directed General Jubal A. Early, now commanding Stonewall Jackson's old corps, to leave the Richmond sector, march swiftly to Lynchburg, drive off a Federal raiding force, strike northward down the Shenadoah, cross the Potomac, and threaten Washington. So daring a move might force Grant to detach men and ease pressure at Petersburg.

Early's Raid on Washington. Early's raid began in mid-June. By swift marching—marching to do credit to Jackson's memory—and hard fighting at Lynchburg and at the Battle of Monocacy, Maryland, July 9, Early reached Washington's ramparts on the 11th. With scarcely 10,000 infantry and few troopers, he could not attack the fortifications, especially since they were being reinforced by men from Meade's army. But Early gained his objective; he scared Lincoln into calling for help from Grant, pinned down at least two Union corps, confused several Northern states, and cleared the Shenandoah of enemy marauders. He did not draw enough bluecoats from Petersburg, but did at least demonstrate that the Rebels still had the power of attack. Confederate troops withdrew from Washington on July 12, but lingered in the Valley. Grant sent General Philip Sheridan to deal with Early, and the last part of 1864 saw a series of bloody encounters between these two determined soldiers. Early fought with few men and much bluff and for a time had the best of it. But Sheridan built up his strength, and when he moved late in the year to finish Early, he had the men and equipment to do it. The last of the old Army of the Valley evaporated under Sheridan's attack at Waynesboro, Virginia, in March, 1865.

Lee's Lines Broken. Early did all that Lee could have expected. Although Marse Robert needed every man in the siege lines, detachment to the Valley paid dividends in food to sustain the main army through much of the last winter. The siege grew in intensity; weather worked terrible hardship on the ill-clad graycoats; railroad routes to the south were cut down to one main line and supplies grew proportionately scant; the officer corps was riddled by attrition and command faltered; men began to desert in tens, then twenties, hundreds as the ranks melted away. Across the grim ditches, the Union army grew steadily larger.

On the second of April, 1865, Grant made his final move. After stretching the siege lines westward along the Appomattox River beyond Lee's capacity to man them, Grant directed a general assault. It began early that Sunday morning and quickly breached the Confederate line. Lee sent word to President Davis that Richmond must be evacuated and began preparations for retreat into North Carolina and a possible link-up with Johnston's remnants, which were retreating in front of Sherman. The retreat proved one long agony. Federals cut off the roads south and forced Lee westward toward Farmville and Lynchburg. Rations grew scarce, then disappeared altogether. None could be found for days, and when a trainload of food did meet the army, a Yankee force broke up the distribution. A sickening surprise encounter during the retreat chopped up an entire Confederate corps and when Lee's Army reached the vicinity of Appomattox Court House, it had barely 23,000 men present for duty.

Lee Surrenders. Lee communicated with Grant concerning surrender, and on Sunday, April 9, 1865, the two opposing leaders met to work out details. Terms were generous, generous enough to win praise from Lee, and he signed them. Grant signed. And a curious hush came over the fields between armies which had been shooting at each other a few hours before and for what seemed endless years. (*See Document No. 20.*)

Last scenes in war are generally fragments, a vignette here and there in a thousand places. But at Appomattox everything really ended. Lee had been made commanding general of Confederate armies, yet properly refused to surrender any army but his own. Still, when he surrendered the greatest of Confederate forces, nothing lingered of the cause save a final meeting between Sherman and Johnston on April 26, a fleeing and poignantly determined President, surrender of Kirby Smith's domain on May 26, and a ruined Southland.

Out of the Rebel lines came the Stonewall Brigade, a tiny bit of the proudest unit in the whole army. These men, these pitiful few, could boast of being with Old Jack himself in all he did and of being in everything since. They were ragged, starved, and unutterably tired—but they were Jackson's men and they marched like they were— straight, closed up, and no straggling. Then, slowly, came the rest of the army. The Yankees, those familiar boys in blue, made no sound, gave no cheer. The Rebels were beaten and it was good that they were, for they were fearsome soldiers who outlasted their cause.

— 6 —

"KING JEFF THE FIRST"

Attitudes Toward Davis. High on every list of reasons for Confederate defeat is Jefferson Davis. He is often pictured as petty, uncompromising, legalistic, brittle, autocratic, as a man whose natural chill fended off friendships, as a poor war leader and a terrible politician. This image comes partly from contemporary enemies, such as Edward A. Pollard, editor of the violently anti-Davis Richmond *Examiner*. The first historian of the Confederacy, Pollard published in 1862 a skillful account of *The First Year of the War*, slanted to show Davis as the engineer of Rebel ruin. The more Pollard thought about Davis during the war, the more convinced he became of the President's dictatorial bent and of his incompetence as an administrator. Rarely did an issue of his paper appear without some acid editorial aimed at the Confederate White House. Robert Barnwell Rhett added to the twisted Davis portrait with venomous columns in the Charleston *Mercury* echoing charges of autocracy.

And, since historians are human and often misled by their sources, the image lasted, even grew in distortion. Present-day views of the embattled President differ in detail but remain essentially unfavorable. A recent biographer, Hudson Strode, is in the midst of a three-volume work presenting Davis in enthusiastic terms, but the opposition is formidable. A good deal of the opposition arises from failure to understand Davis' strengths and weaknesses as administrator and politician.

Davis as Administrator. Many of Davis' deeds show him to have been a poor administrator. Never did he learn to delegate sufficient authority to subordinates, and this meant that he spent endless time on small details which could have been easily handled by others. Apparently he felt that he knew better than anyone else how to do all the jobs connected with the Executive Branch. Witness his constant interference in affairs of the War Department, interference which caused several good Secretaries to resign rather than be mere rubber stamps. But he did make some attempts to delegate responsibility for military operations by creating geographical and theater commands —attempts which indicate he learned under pressure that all could not be run from Richmond.

In personnel management, Davis showed a hardheaded dedication to friends he put in office. This unswerving loyalty often led him to retain in the government civilian and military leaders whose services were at best dubious and at worst disastrous. Any criticism of a friend might provoke the President to a lasting vendetta, a serious defect which showed his inability to accept disagreement or criticism.

Perhaps the most important quality of a good administrator is a capacity to adjust to new situations. Davis' legalistic turn of mind made him slow to adjust, and left him sometimes with ideas and views outmoded by crisis. But he learned with experience and developed some pliability —not enough, perhaps, but some. He forced himself to modify strategy as the need bore in upon him, and perhaps the best indication of his adaptibility was his shift from state righter to Confederate nationalist. This political about-face came hard, but Davis soon saw the need for strong government and worked to achieve it. In some things, of course, he remained essentially brittle. For instance, he never changed his mind about the illegality of the Union blockade, and although reluctantly forced to condone government efforts to breach the cordon, he continued to parade statistics before the world in a futile effort to prove his point.

For what he learned of the nature of war, for what he did to transform an agrarian South into a moderately centralized bureaucracy, Davis deserves credit. Although he knew that conscription, impressment, commercial nationalization, an income tax, would bring him the hatred of thousands, he argued tirelessly for these measures as essential to a total war effort. He probably failed to use all the executive power at his disposal and doubtless stayed too close to the Confederate constitution, but he was nonetheless a strong president.

Davis as Politician. Many Confederates thought they had a visionary for a Chief Executive, a man lost in constitutional theory. But Davis defied easy analysis—he showed visionary tendencies one day, cold calculation the next. Although he did cherish some roseate ideas about democratic institutions and about ultimate victory, he could be intensely practical at times. In 1864, for example, when disaffection spread through parts of Georgia, North Carolina, Alabama, and Mississippi, Davis fought it grimly. Faced with treasonable organizations, peace societies, and even secessionist sentiment in Georgia, he worked shrewdly to steal the disunionist thunder by showing that the only choice open to the South was independence or subjugation. To prove his contention, and at the same time to silence whispers that he refused to talk peace because of some lurking death urge, he agreed to the Hampton Roads Conference in February, 1865.

Lincoln and Secretary Seward met Vice-President Stephens and two other Confederate commissioners aboard the *River Queen* at Hampton Roads, Virginia, on February 3. Davis had guessed the outcome, and he was right: Lincoln insisted on reunion, emancipation, and demobilization of Rebel armies. Even Little Alec, chronic carper, had to admit that the North showed no willingness to compromise on the basic issues of the conflict, and that Davis had not deceived the people in urging hard war as the only guarantee of independence. Hampton Roads proved a deft piece of presidential strategy for Confederate spirit revived and the South made last ditch efforts to carry on. Davis had the personal satisfaction of noting the confusion of his enemies—but satisfaction must have been cold and bitter midst the shambles of the South.

Canny and guileful in maneuver against personal foes, Davis showed these same qualities in statecraft. At the outset he understood the necessity of convincing the "upper South" that it must join the Confederacy and he used commercial, economic, and social blandishments, along with appeals to enlightened self-interest, in a successful campaign to win North Carolina and Tennessee. Later he wooed Kentucky with words of friendship and liberation. These manipulations to achieve "natural" Confederate borders give evidence of Davis' growing maturity as a statesman.

Added evidence comes from the way in which he built a government and military forces. With sure, deft strokes he fashioned the cabinet, mobilized the manpower and economy of the South, and planned a war effort which grew in size and strength. Probably no other administrator could have constructed the Confederate government and made it last four years.

Davis' achievement is the more remarkable in view of his limitations as a politician. His demeanor, dignity, and hauteur inhibited his political charm; and for the most part he had little understanding of constituents and their demands. Stump speaking, cider quaffing, tobacco spitting, all the low trappings of Jacksonian democracy, Davis rose above them. Instead of winning people to him, he rested content with stating a logical case—a dubious kind of political magnetism.

He suffered the misfortune of having things too easy at first. Secession enthusiasm gave way to a façade of Southern unity which lasted through most of 1861 and lent an impression of satisfaction with Davis' performance. Considerable unrest lurked beneath the surface, but Davis was not forced by disaster to doff his superiority, to charm and wheedle support for his administration. A few friends knew his wit, his warmth, but he apparently felt that "politicking" was somehow out of place in public relations. Consequently, as he proclaimed, preached, and commanded his war, he alienated friends, large segments of the Confederate population, and a growing number in Congress.

The Confederate Congress. Davis' deficiencies as a politician were most starkly revealed in his relations with the Confederate Congress. Charged by the Constitution with providing executive leadership, he lived up to the letter of the charter. His messages show, however, how his patience eroded as the war progressed. At first he addressed Congress with due deference, with the respect a former U.S. Senator would show to a legislative body. But when he talked business, discussed his program, or recommended legislation, he could never avoid a pompous, condescending tone which conveyed an air of disdain. As the war continued and as Congress became disenchanted with some administration measures, Davis' language grew sharper and less polite. Finally a carping, accusative note appeared, and when the Confederacy tottered toward collapse the President scolded at Congressional failures.

Be it said for Congress that it bore presidential preaching and berating with considerable good grace. In time, of course, a sizable segment of Congress turned against Davis and the war. But for almost three years the President could count on a fair hearing and a good measure of success. This is mildly surprising in face of the commonly accepted view of the Confederate Congress as a petty, quarrelsome, crude aggregation of political nincompoops. But recent studies indicate that Congress boasted a good deal of talent. Although most members were products of an agrarian society and hence had a limited view of modern war, they learned as time passed and forced themselves to legislate a total effort. The President did not always provide constructive or consistent leadership, but Congress made honest efforts to do what he asked. Even though many members leveled a good deal of criticism at parts of the Administration's war program, Congress overrode a Davis veto only once, and on a minor matter.

Congressional Nationalism. This is not to imply that Congress passively accepted ill-treatment by the President. Numbers of congressmen and senators early developed a cordial dislike for Davis and took special pleasure in puncturing his pomposity. They soon saw they could goad him by criticism, by threatened investigations of his administration, and by refusing to grant some powers he sought. When, for instance, he asked for permission to suspend the writ of habeas corpus and declare martial law following the loss of Forts Henry and Donelson and during Federal approaches to Richmond, Congress seemed to take pleasure in restricting the authority in time and place. And when Congress heard that Confederate generals were declaring martial law without authority, Davis' enemies gleefully blamed the autocracy of the government. In

1865, after fear and hatred of "King Jeff the First" broke bounds, a desperate Administration plea to suspend the writ as a feeble means of coping with collapse was summarily rejected.

But these examples of petty personal hostility were offset by many examples of Congressional cooperation. Although members knew they would incur popular wrath by enacting the centralist military and economic parts of Davis' war program, Congress passed these stringent measures. Why did an irritated and bitter Congress so often do Dictator Davis' bidding? Was it because of a spirit of selfless patriotism or because Congress could offer nothing better? Both factors form part of the answer, but Davis had his way largely because a hard core of nationalist members stuck by their old principles of sound money, strong government, and law and order. Former Whigs aligned with nationalist Democrats to give Congress a flavor of nationalism, although they could not always overcome the opposition of such diehard Davis haters as Senator Louis T. Wigfall and Congressman Henry S. Foote. But even after the significant anti-administration victories in the congressional elections of 1863, most hard war measures still were supported by these Whiggish gentlemen who retained a healthy respect for government. Many of these men had been Unionists who accepted the sanctity of secession and "went with their state." Among this important group were Benjamin H. Hill of Georgia, Ethelbert Barksdale of Mississippi, and Arthur Colyar of Tennessee.

Davis and State Righters. If Davis had some little influence in Congress, he had virtually none with such state rights governors as Joe Brown and Zeb Vance. Brown's chronic discontent erupted with the first conscription act and for a time he waged a lonesome fight against military despotism in Richmond. Late in 1862, Vance won the North Carolina governor's chair on a war and state rights platform, and immediately became a Brown ally. Brown later gained the added assistance of a state rights Georgia junto, with himself, Alexander Stephens, and Robert Toombs as members. Toombs, frustrated politician and disgruntled former Confederate brigadier, lent his vast influence and forceful language to the anti-administration campaign. And by 1863 the Vice President of the Confederate States had deserted the government to sulk in Georgia and issue moody statements prophesying dictatorship and doom. This unholy threesome probably gave more aid and comfort to the enemy than any other group in the South. Curiously enough, all three fancied themselves great patriots. And in their twisted way, they were: Toombs never lost his zealot's verve for the cause; Stephens' sunken eyes flashed fire yet when he talked of Southern nationalism; Brown declared that he rebelled to prevent centralization of government and would hold to that purpose. The interesting thing is that Brown and some other governors who prated against centralization became dictators within their own states in order to resist Davis' dictatorship.

Could Davis have done anything to pacify these Confederate rightists? Given the personalities involved, probably not. But he might have done better had he had some political sophistication. He tried to persuade and cajole these men, but when that failed, he fell back on his acid pen—and his sharply critical letters were notorious instruments of alienation.

Davis and the National Spirit. One of the real tragedies of Davis' career is that he wanted to reach people, to lift his cause on stirring words and sustain the war spirit. But frozen by shyness and caste, he had no gift for inspiring the public. Several times he tried to overcome his personality and to forge a Confederate national spirit, and each time he failed. By the middle of 1863 morale declined dangerously; many Southerners forgot the "why" of the war; the will to go on ebbed.

Davis used what mass media were available to pump up national determination, but newspapers were often hostile and always individualistic in their ideas on the war. The President spoke frequently through his messages to Congress, but these were uninspired and the long, dull columns they occupied in the papers probably went largely unread. Thrice during the war he departed Richmond to carry his program to the Deep South, and in speeches before several mass meetings and before the Mississippi Legislature he almost reached eloquence—sincerity was his greatest asset in this sort of appearance. Parts of his program were carried to the people by some members of Congress who took to the hustings in various sections of the South. Apparently these speeches were momentarily effective, but audiences were limited and memories short. Government propaganda—as it would be called today—reached the people most effectively from the pulpit. Even so, the messages reached comparatively few. Soldiers finally forgot, many of them, what great issues had pulled them from home and family and cast them to the rigors of the field. Some, of course, recalled Yankee pillaging, others had grim vendettas to honor, but toward the last most of the tattered battalions stayed only because men did what they had to do, and because General Lee still led them.

The End. Davis stayed because he had a will of iron and deathless devotion to the Confederacy. The last months were one long agony for him. On every side he could see growing desperation and felt the gradual withering of governmental power. He reacted typically: while the South disintegrated, while thousands resigned themselves to losing the war, Davis' faith in the future revived and burned fiercer than ever. At a mass rally in Richmond's African Church on February 6, 1865, he gave his greatest speech and his eloquence kindled a flickering afterglow of hope. But the spark died swiftly as Sherman knifed through the Carolinas and Grant's lines extended at Petersburg.

Congress yielded to panic, and in a pell-mell rush to get right with the Confederacy repealed much war legislation during the last days of the final session, sniped at the President, resisted his advice, and virtually surrendered to the governors. But on one key issue Davis had his way; Congress did authorize the arming of slaves. Surely this reveals more forcefully than anything else the true war aim of the South. Slavery may have been the Confederacy's cornerstone, but independence remained its heart's desire.

At the last, after Lee took his army on its heroic march to Appomattox and to history, Davis fled Richmond and went South with a coterie of officials, friends, and a cavalry guard. From Danville, Virginia, he issued his last message to revive the Confederacy, and it did him and his country proud. (*See Document No. 21.*) But nothing was left—no spirit, no men, no supplies, no munitions. The President fell into Federal hands near Irwinsville, Georgia, on May 10, the ignominy of capture being offset somewhat by Davis' dauntless dignity.

THE LOST CAUSE

One of the most fascinating questions of American history is why was the Lost Cause lost? Answers usually split along sectional lines. Northern historians frequently see victory as the inevitable result of a struggle between righteous Yankee freemen and Rebels enfeebled by the sin of slavery. Southerners deny that slavery constituted a fatal flaw. During and after the war Southern historians argued that the Confederacy contended from the outset against hopeless odds, and a few pointed out that internal problems helped increase the odds. More recent Southern students have focused attention on life behind the Confederate lines in an attempt to find out how the Rebels beat themselves.

Frank L. Owsley in *State Rights in the Confederacy* (1925) laid the blame for defeat at the door of state rights; he maintained that the divisive force of unbridled localism crippled the central government from the beginning of the war. Other scholars have listed inner dissension, the blockade, loss of the will to win, failure to appreciate Northern affection for the Union, failure of public information and consequent decline in morale, misjudgment of Europe's position, and the tide of history in the nineteenth century as reasons for Southern defeat. Still others have added poor administrative techniques, misuse of the Negro population, unsound military strategy, truncated centralization, and Jefferson Davis' incompetence to the list.

All of these factors had some effect on the outcome of the war. But those who accept them as the main reasons for defeat overlook the cold fact of Confederate performance. For four terrible years the South sustained a total war, mobilized and managed a modern industrial effort, and lost utterly. The very totality of defeat is evidence of maximum effort. The conclusion is inescapable that even with all the weaknesses listed, the South had sufficient genius, will, and wherewithal to fight a war of limited duration. But there was the rub: how long could it survive in the first modern war of attrition? Resources were mobilized more rapidly and perhaps more thoroughly than in the North, but by 1863 the South had shot its bolt. Resources failed the test of time. Those they had the Confederates used to the utmost and beyond. But when everything began to give out, when the Confederacy became hagridden by poverty and privation, a general decay set in which progressively paralyzed the armies, the economy, politics, society, and which destroyed morale. The Confederate States was first exhausted, then defeated.

Part II

DOCUMENTS

— Document No. 1 —

SOUTH CAROLINA ORDINANCE OF SECESSION, DECEMBER 20, 1860[1]

South Carolina awaited news of the election of 1860 with considerable excitement. Most South Carolinians felt that the election of "Black Republican" Lincoln would mark the end of the Federal Union, and when definite news of his victory arrived in the state, a convention was called on December 17, 1860, to consider relations with the United States. On December 20, the convention unanimously adopted an ordinance of secession.

An Ordinance to Dissolve the Union between the State of South Carolina and other States united with her under the compact entitled the Constitution of the United States of America:

We, the people of the State of South Carolina, in Convention assembled, do declare and ordain, and it is hereby declared and ordained, that the ordinance adopted by us in Convention, on the 23rd day of May, in the year of our Lord 1788, whereby the Constitution of the United States of America was ratified, and also all Acts and parts of Acts of the General Assembly of this State ratifying the amendments of the said Constitution, are hereby repealed, and that the union now subsisting between South Carolina and other States under the name of the United States of America is hereby dissolved.

[1] From Frank Moore, ed., *The Rebellion Record* (12 vols., New York, 1862-1871,) I, 2.

— Document No. 2 —

THE CONSTITUTION OF THE CONFEDERATE STATES OF AMERICA, MARCH 11, 1861 [2]

The Confederate Constitution resembled the old United States document in most respects, but contained some differences and improvements. The African slave trade was prohibited. The President held office for six years, but was not eligible for re-election; he had authority to veto separate items in appropriation bills; under the Confederate charter he had more power than the President of the United States. Congress had its wings clipped by a provision prohibiting the appropriation of money without specific request from the Executive branch. Some hints of the Parliamentary system appear in the document. And, significantly, the Constitution is the supreme law of the land.

✿   ✿   ✿

We, the people of the Confederate States, each State acting in its sovereign and independent character, in order to form a permanent government, establish justice, insure domestic tranquillity, and secure the blessings of liberty to ourselves and our posterity—invoking the favor and guidance of Almighty God—do ordain and establish this Constitution for the Confederate States of America.

ART. I

SEC. 1.—All legislative powers herein delegated shall be vested in a Congress of the Confederate States, which shall consist of a Senate and House of Representatives.

[2] James M. Matthews, ed., *Statutes at Large of the Provisional Government of the Confederate States of America* (Richmond, 1864), pp. 11-23.

SEC. 2. (1) The House of Representatives shall be . . . chosen every second year by the people of the several States; and the electors in each State shall be citizens of the Confederate States, and have the qualifications requisite for electors of the most numerous branch of the State Legislature; but no person of foreign birth, not a citizen of the Confederate States, shall be allowed to vote for any officer, civil or political, State or Federal.

(2) No person shall be a Representative who shall not have attained the age of twenty-five years, and be a citizen of the Confederate States, and who shall not, when elected, be an inhabitant of that State in which he shall be chosen.

(3) Representatives and direct taxes shall be apportioned among the several States which may be included within this Confederacy, according to their respective numbers, which shall be determined by adding to the whole number of free persons, including those bound to service for a term of years, and excluding Indians not taxed, three-fifths of all slaves. The actual enumeration shall be made within three years after the first meeting of the Congress of the Confederate States, and within every subsequent term of ten years, in such manner as they shall by law direct. The number of Representatives shall not exceed one for every fifty thousand, but each State shall have at least one Representative; and until such enumeration shall be made the State of South Carolina shall be entitled to choose six; the State of Georgia ten; the State of Alabama nine; the State of Florida two; the State of Mississippi seven; the State of Louisiana six; and the State of Texas six.

(4) When vacancies happen in the representation of any State, the Executive authority thereof shall issue writs of election to fill such vacancies.

(5) The House of Representatives shall choose their Speaker and other officers; and shall have the sole power of impeachment; except that any judicial or other federal officer resident and acting solely within the limits of any State, may be impeached by a vote of two-thirds of both branches of the Legislature thereof.

SEC. 3. (1) The Senate of the Confederate States shall be composed of two Senators from each State, chosen for six years by the Legislature thereof, at the regular session next immediately preceding the commencement of the term of service; and each Senator shall have one vote.

(2) Immediately after they shall be assembled, in consequence of the first election, they shall be divided as equally as may be into three classes. The seats of the Senators of the first class shall be vacated at the expiration of the second year; of the second class at the expiration of the fourth year; and of the third class at the expiration of the sixth year; so that one-third may be chosen every second year; and if vacancies happen by resignation or otherwise during the recess of the Legislature of any State, the Executive thereof may make temporary appointments until the next meeting of the Legislature, which shall then fill such vacancies.

(3) No person shall be a Senator, who shall not have attained the age of thirty years, and be a citizen of the Confederate States; and who shall not, when elected, be an inhabitant of the State for which he shall be chosen.

(4) The Vice-President of the Confederate States shall be President of the Senate, but shall have no vote, unless they be equally divided.

(5) The Senate shall choose their other officers, and also a President pro tempore, in the absence of the Vice-President, or when he shall exercise the office of President of the Confederate States.

(6) The Senate shall have sole power to try all impeachments. When sitting for that purpose they shall be on oath or affirmation. When the President of the Confederate States is tried, the Chief Justice shall preside; and no person shall be convicted without the concurrence of two-thirds of the members present.

(7) Judgment in cases of impeachment shall not extend further than removal from office, and disqualification to hold and enjoy any office of honor, trust, or profit, under the Confederate States; but the party convicted shall, nevertheless, be liable and subject to indictment, trial, judgment, and punishment according to law.

SEC. 4. (1) The times, places, and manner of holding elections for Senators and Representatives, shall be prescribed in each State by the Legislature thereof, subject to the provisions of this Constitution; but the Congress may, at any time, by law, make or alter such regulations, except as to the times and places of choosing Senators.

(2) The Congress shall assemble at least once in every year; and such meeting shall be on the first Monday in December, unless they shall, by law, appoint a different day.

SEC. 5. (1) Each House shall be the judge of the elections, returns, and qualifications of its own members, and a majority of each shall constitute a quorum to do business; but a smaller number may adjourn from day to day, and may be authorized to compel the attendance of absent members, in such manner and under such penalties as each House may provide.

(2) Each House may determine the rules of its proceedings, punish its members for disorderly behavior, and, with the concurrence of two-thirds of the whole number, expel a member.

(3) Each House shall keep a journal of its proceedings, and from time to time publish the same, excepting such parts as may in their judgment require secrecy, and the ayes and nays of the members of either House, on any question, shall, at the desire of one-fifth of those present, be entered on the journal.

(4) Neither House, during the session of Congress, shall, without the consent of the other, adjourn for more than three days, nor to any other place than that in which the two Houses shall be sitting.

SEC. 6. (1) The Senators and Representatives shall receive a compensation for their services, to be ascertained by law, and paid out of the Treasury of the Confederate States. They shall, in all cases except treason and breach of the peace, be privileged from arrest during their attendance at the session of their respective Houses, and in going to and returning from the same; and for any speech or debate in either House, they shall not be questioned in any other place.

(2) No Senator or Representative shall, during the time for which he was elected, be appointed to any civil office under the authority of the Confederate States, which shall have been created, or the emoluments whereof shall have been increased during such time; and no person holding any office under the Confederate States shall be a

member of either House during his continuance in office. But Congress may, by law, grant to the principal officer in each of the Executive Departments a seat upon the floor of either House, with the privilege of discussing any measure appertaining to his department.

SEC. 7. (1) All bills for raising revenue shall originate in the House of Representatives; but the Senate may propose or concur with amendments as on other bills.

(2) Every bill which shall have passed both Houses shall, before it becomes a law, be presented to the President of the Confederate States; if he approve he shall sign it; but if not, he shall return it with his objections to that House in which it shall have originated, who shall enter the objections at large on their journal, and proceed to reconsider it. If, after such reconsideration, two-thirds of that House shall agree to pass the bill, it shall be sent, together with the objections, to the other House, by which it shall likewise be reconsidered, and if approved by two-thirds of that House, it shall become a law. But in all such cases, the votes of both Houses shall be determined by yeas and nays, and the names of the persons voting for and against the bill shall be entered on the journal of each House respectively. If any bill shall not be returned by the President within ten days (Sundays excepted) after it shall have been presented to him, the same shall be a law, in like manner as if he had signed it, unless the Congress, by their adjournment, prevent its return; in which case it shall not be a law. The President may approve any appropriation and disapprove any other appropriation in the same bill. In such case he shall, in signing the bill, designate the appropriations disapproved; and shall return a copy of such appropriations, with his objections, to the House in which the bill shall have originated; and the same proceedings shall then be had as in case of other bills disapproved by the President.

(3) Every order, resolution, or vote, to which the concurrence of both Houses may be necessary (except on a question of adjournment) shall be presented to the President of the Confederate States; and before the same shall take effect shall be approved by him; or being disapproved by him, shall be repassed by two-thirds of both Houses,

according to the rules and limitations prescribed in case of a bill.

SEC. 8.—The Congress shall have power—(1) To lay and collect taxes, duties, imposts, and excises, for revenue necessary to pay the debts, provide for the common defence, and carry on the Government of the Confederate States; but no bounties shall be granted from the treasury; nor shall any duties or taxes on importations from foreign nations be laid to promote or foster any branch of industry; and all duties, imposts, and excises shall be uniform throughout the Confederate States.

(2) To borrow money on the credit of the Confederate States.

(3) To regulate commerce with foreign nations, and among the several States, and with the Indian tribes; but neither this nor any other clause contained in the Constitution shall be construed to delegate the power to Congress to appropriate money for any internal improvement intended to facilitate commerce; except for the purpose of furnishing lights, beacons, and buoys, and other aids to navigation upon the coasts, and the improvement of harbors, and the removing of obstructions in river navigation, in all which cases, such duties shall be laid on the navigation facilitated thereby, as may be necessary to pay the costs and expenses thereof.

(4) To establish uniform laws of naturalization, and uniform laws on the subject of bankruptcies throughout the Confederate States, but no law of Congress shall discharge any debt contracted before the passage of the same.

(5) To coin money, regulate the value thereof, and of foreign coin, and fix the standard of weights and measures.

(6) To provide for the punishment of counterfeiting the securities and current coin of the Confederate States.

(7) To establish post-offices and post-routes; but the expenses of the Post-office Department, after the first day of March, in the year of our Lord eighteen hundred and sixty-three, shall be paid out of its own revenues.

(8) To promote the progress of science and useful arts, by securing for limited times to authors and inventors the exclusive right to their respective writings and discoveries.

(9) To constitute tribunals inferior to the Supreme Court.

(10) To define and punish piracies and felonies committed on the high seas, and offences against the law of nations.

(11) To declare war, grant letters of marque and reprisal, and make rules concerning captures on land and water.

(12) To raise and support armies; but no appropriation of money to that use shall be for a longer term than two years.

(13) To provide and maintain a navy.

(14) To make rules for government and regulation of the land and naval forces.

(15) To provide for calling forth the militia to execute the laws of the Confederate States; suppress insurrections, and repel invasions.

(16) To provide for organizing, arming, and disciplining the militia, and for governing such part of them as may be employed in the service of the Confederate States; reserving to the States, respectively, the appointment of the officers, and the authority of training the militia according to the discipline prescribed by Congress.

(17) To exercise exclusive legislation, in all cases whatsoever, over such district (not exceeding ten miles square) as may, by cession of one or more States, and the acceptance of Congress, become the seat of the Government of the Confederate States; and to exercise a like authority over all places purchased by the consent of the Legislature of the State in which the same shall be, for the erection of forts, magazines, arsenals, dock-yards, and other needful buildings, and

(18) To make all laws which shall be necessary and proper for carrying into execution the foregoing powers, and all other powers vested by this Constitution in the Government of the Confederate States, or in any department or officer thereof.

Sec. 9. (1) The importation of negroes of the African race, from any foreign country, other than the slaveholding States or Territories of the United States of America, is hereby forbidden; and Congress is required to pass such laws as shall effectually prevent the same.

(2) Congress shall also have power to prohibit the in-

troduction of slaves from any State not a member of, or Territory not belonging to, this Confederacy.

(3) The privilege of the writ of habeas corpus shall not be suspended, unless when in cases of rebellion or invasion the public safety may require it.

(4) No bill of attainder, ex post facto law, or law denying or impairing the right of property in negro slaves shall be passed.

(5) No capitation or other direct tax shall be laid unless in proportion to the census or enumeration hereinbefore directed to be taken.

(6) No tax or duty shall be laid on articles exported from any State, except by a vote of two-thirds of both Houses.

(7) No preference shall be given by any regulation of commerce or revenue to the ports of one State over those of another.

(8) No money shall be drawn from the treasury but in consequence of appropriations made by law; and a regular statement and account of the receipts and expenditures of all public money shall be published from time to time.

(9) Congress shall appropriate no money from the treasury except by a vote of two-thirds of both Houses, taken by yeas and nays, unless it be asked and estimated for by some one of the heads of departments, and submitted to Congress by the President; or for the purpose of paying its own expenses and contingencies; or for the payment of claims against the Confederate States, the justice of which shall have been judicially declared by a tribunal for the investigation of claims against the Government, which it is hereby made the duty of Congress to establish.

(10) All bills appropriating money shall specify in federal currency the exact amount of each appropriation and the purposes for which it is made; and Congress shall grant no extra compensation to any public contractor, officer, agent, or servant, after such contract shall have been made or such service rendered.

(11) No title of nobility shall be granted by the Confederate States; and no person holding any office of profit

or trust under them shall, without the consent of the Congress, accept of any present, emolument, office, or title of any kind whatever, from any king, prince, or foreign state.

(12) Congress shall make no law respecting an establishment of religion, or prohibiting the free exercise thereof; or abridging the freedom of speech or of the press; or the right of the people peaceably to assemble and petition the Government for a redress of grievances.

(13) A well-regulated militia being necessary to the security of a free State, the right of the people to keep and bear arms shall not be infringed.

(14) No soldier shall, in time of peace, be quartered in any house without the consent of the owner; nor in time of war, but in a manner to be prescribed by law.

(15) The right of the people to be secure in their persons, houses, papers, and effects, against unreasonable searches and seizures, shall not be violated; and no warrant shall issue but upon probable cause, supported by oath or affirmation, and particularly describing the place to be searched, and the person or things to be seized.

(16) No person shall be held to answer for a capital or otherwise infamous crime, unless on a presentment or indictment of a grand jury, except in cases arising in the land or naval forces, or in the militia, when in actual service, in time of war, or public danger; nor shall any person be subject for the same offence to be twice put in jeopardy of life or limb; nor be compelled in any criminal case to be a witness against himself; nor be deprived of life, liberty, or property, without due process of law; nor shall private property be taken for public use without just compensation.

(17) In all criminal prosecutions the accused shall enjoy the right to a speedy and public trial, by an impartial jury of the State and district wherein the crime shall have been committed, which district shall have been previously ascertained by law, and to be informed of the nature and cause of the accusation; to be confronted with the witnesses against him; to have compulsory process for obtaining witnesses in his favor; and to have the assistance of counsel for his defence.

(18) In suits at common law, where the value in con-

troversy shall exceed twenty dollars, the right of trial by jury shall be preserved; and no fact so tried by a jury shall be otherwise reexamined in any court of the Confederacy, than according to the rules of common law.

(19) Excessive bail shall not be required, nor excessive fines imposed, nor cruel and unusual punishment inflicted.

(20) Every law, or resolution having the force of law, shall relate to but one subject, and that shall be expressed in the title.

SEC. 10. (1) No State shall enter into any treaty, alliance, or confederation; grant letters of marque and reprisal; coin money; make any thing but gold and silver coin a tender in payment of debts; pass any bill of attainder, or ex post facto law, or law impairing the obligation of contracts; or grant any title of nobility.

(2) No State shall, without the consent of Congress, lay any imposts or duties on imports or exports, except what may be absolutely necessary for executing its inspection laws; and the net produce of all duties and imposts, laid by any State on imports or exports, shall be for the use of the Treasury of the Confederate States; and all such laws shall be subject to the revision and control of Congress.

(3) No State shall, without the consent of Congress, lay any duty on tonnage, except on sea-going vessels, for the improvement of its rivers and harbors navigated by the said vessels; but such duties shall not conflict with any treaties of the Confederate States with foreign nations; and any surplus revenue, thus derived, shall, after making such improvement, be paid into the common treasury; nor shall any State keep troops or ships of war in time of peace, enter into any agreement or compact with another State, or with a foreign power, or engage in war, unless actually invaded, or in such imminent danger as will not admit of delay. But when any river divides or flows through two or more States, they may enter into compacts with each other to improve the navigation thereof.

ART. II

SEC. 1. (1) The Executive power shall be vested in a President of the Confederate States of America. He and the Vice-President shall hold their offices for the term of six years; but the President shall not be reeligible. The President and Vice-President shall be elected as follows:

(2) Each State shall appoint, in such manner as the Legislature thereof may direct, a number of electors equal to the whole number of Senators and Representatives to which the State may be entitled in the Congress; but no Senator or Representative, or person holding an office of trust or profit under the Confederate States, shall be appointed an elector.

(3) The electors shall meet in their respective States and vote by ballot for President and Vice-President, one of whom, at least shall not be an inhabitant of the same State with themselves; they shall name in their ballots the person voted for as President, and in distinct ballots the person voted for as Vice-President, and they shall make distinct lists of all persons voted for as President, and of all persons voted for as Vice-President, and of the number of votes for each; which list they shall sign, and certify, and transmit, sealed, to the . . . government of the Confederate States, directed to the President of the Senate. The President of the Senate shall, in the presence of the Senate and House of Representatives, open all the certificates, and the votes shall then be counted; the person having the greatest number of votes for President shall be the President, if such number be a majority of the whole number of electors appointed; and if no person shall have such a majority, then, from the persons having the highest numbers, not exceeding three, on the list of those voted for as President, the House of Representatives shall choose immediately, by ballot, the President. But, in choosing the President, the votes shall be taken by States, the representation from each State having one vote; a quorum for this purpose shall consist of a member or members from two-thirds of the States, and a majority of all the States shall be necessary to a choice. And if the House of Representatives shall not choose a President, whenever the right of choice shall devolve upon them, before the fourth day of March next following, then the Vice-President shall act as President, as in case of the death, or other constitutional disability of the President.

(4) The person having the greatest number of votes as

Vice-President shall be the Vice-President, if such number be a majority of the whole number of electors appointed; and if no person have a majority, then from the two highest numbers on the list, the Senate shall choose the Vice-President; a quorum for the purpose shall consist of two-thirds of the whole number of Senators, and a majority of the whole number shall be necessary for a choice.

(5) But no person constitutionally ineligible to the office of President shall be eligible to that of Vice-President of the Confederate States.

(6) The Congress may determine the time of choosing the electors, and the day on which they shall give their votes; which day shall be the same throughout the Confederate States.

(7) No person except a natural born citizen of the Confederate States, or a citizen thereof, at the time of the adoption of this Constitution, or a citizen thereof born in the United States prior to the 20th of December, 1860, shall be eligible to the office of President; neither shall any person be eligible to that office who shall not have attained the age of thirty-five years, and been fourteen years a resident within the limits of the Confederate States, as they may exist at the time of his election.

(8) In case of the removal of the President from office, or of his death, resignation, or inability to discharge the powers and duties of the said office, the same shall devolve on the Vice-President; and the Congress may, by law, provide for the case of the removal, death, resignation, or inability both of the President and the Vice-President, declaring what officer shall then act as President, and such officer shall then act accordingly until the disability be removed or a President shall be elected.

(9) The President shall, at stated times, receive for his services a compensation, which shall neither be increased nor diminished during the period for which he shall have been elected; and he shall not receive within that period any other emolument from the Confederate States, or any of them.

(10) Before he enters on the execution [of the duties] of his office, he shall take the following oath or affirmation:

"I do solemnly swear (or affirm) that I will faithfully execute the office of President of the Confederate States, and will, to the best of my ability, preserve, protect, and defend the Constitution thereof."

Sec. 2. (1) The President shall be commander-in-chief of the army and navy of the Confederate States, and of the militia of the several States, when called into the actual service of the Confederate States; he may require the opinion, in writing, of the principal officer in each of the Executive Departments, upon any subject relating to the duties of their respective offices; and he shall have power to grant reprieves and pardons for offences against the Confederate States, except in cases of impeachment.

(2) He shall have power, by and with the advice and consent of the Senate, to make treaties, provided two-thirds of the Senators present concur; and he shall nom-inate, and, by and with the advice and consent of the Senate, shall appoint ambassadors, other public ministers, and consuls, Judges of the Supreme Court, and all other officers of the Confederate States, whose appointments are not herein otherwise provided for, and which shall be es-tablished by law; but the Congress may by law vest the appointment of such inferior officers, as they think proper, in the President alone, in the courts of law, or in the heads of departments.

(3) The principal officer in each of the Executive De-partments, and all persons connected with the diplomatic service, may be removed from office at the pleasure of the President. All other civil officers of the Executive Depart-ments may be removed at any time by the President, or other appointing power, when their services are unneces-sary, or for dishonesty, incapacity, inefficiency, miscon-duct, or neglect of duty; and when so removed, the removal shall be reported to the Senate, together with the reasons therefor.

(4) The President shall have power to fill all vacancies that may happen during the recess of the Senate, by granting commissions which shall expire at the end of the next session; but no person rejected by the Senate shall be reappointed to the same office during their ensuing recess.

Sec. 3. (1) The President shall, from time to time, give

to the Congress information of the state of the Confederacy, and recommend to their consideration such measures as he shall judge necessary and expedient; he may, on extraordinary occasions, convene both Houses, or either of them; and, in case of disagreement between them, with respect to the time of adjournment he may adjourn them to such time as he shall think proper; he shall receive ambassadors and other public ministers; he shall take care that the laws be faithfully executed, and shall commission all the officers of the Confederate States.

SEC. 4. (1) The President and Vice-President, and all Civil officers of the Confederate States, shall be removed from office on impeachment for, or conviction of, treason, bribery, or other high crimes and misdemeanors.

ART. III

SEC. 1. (1) The judicial power of the Confederate States shall be vested in one Supreme Court, and in such inferior courts as the Congress may from time to time ordain and establish. The judges, both of the Supreme and inferior courts, shall hold their offices during good behavior, and shall, at stated times, receive for their services a compensation, which shall not be diminished during their continuance in office. . . .

ART. IV

SEC. 1. (1) Full faith and credit shall be given in each State to the public acts, records, and judicial proceedings of every other State. And the Congress may, by general laws, prescribe the manner in which such acts, records, and proceedings shall be proved, and the effect thereof.

SEC. 2. (1) The citizens of each State shall be entitled to all the privileges and immunities of citizens of the several States, and shall have the right of transit and sojourn in any State of this Confederacy, with their slaves and other property; and the right of property in said slaves shall not be thereby impaired.

(2) A person charged in any State with treason, felony, or other crime against the laws of such State, who shall flee from justice, and be found in another State, shall, on demand of the executive authority of the State from

which he fled, be delivered up to be removed to the State having jurisdiction of the crime.

(3) No slave or other person held to service or labor in any State or Territory of the Confederate States, under the laws thereof, escaping or [un]lawfully carried into another, shall, in consequence of any law or regulation therein, be discharged from such service or labor; but shall be delivered up on claim of the party to whom such slave belongs, or to whom such service or labor may be due.

SEC. 3. (1) Other States may be admitted into this Confederacy by a vote of two-thirds of the whole House of Representatives, and two-thirds of the Senate, the Senate voting by States; but no new State shall be formed or erected within the jurisdiction of any other State; nor any State be formed by the junction of two or more States, or parts of States, without the consent of the Legislatures of the States concerned as well as of the Congress.

(2) The Congress shall have power to dispose of and make all needful rules and regulations concerning the property of the Confederate States, including the lands thereof.

(3) The Confederate States may acquire new territory; and Congress shall have power to legislate and provide governments for the inhabitants of all territory belonging to the Confederate States, lying without the limits of the several States, and may permit them, at such times, and in such manner as it may by law provide, to form States to be admitted into the Confederacy. In all such territory, the institution of negro slavery, as it now exists in the Confederate States, shall be recognized and protected by Congress and by the territorial government; and the inhabitants of the several Confederate States and Territories shall have the right to take to such territory any slaves lawfully held by them in any of the States or Territories of the Confederate States.

(4) The Confederate States shall guarantee to every State that now is or hereafter may become a member of this Confederacy, a Republican form of Government, and shall protect each of them against invasion; and on application of the Legislature, (or of the Executive when the Legislature is not in session,) against domestic violence.

ART. V

SEC. 1. (1) Upon the demand of any three States, legally assembled in their several Conventions, the Congress shall summon a Convention of all the States, to take into consideration such amendments to the Constitution as the said States shall concur in suggesting at the time when the said demand is made; and should any of the proposed amendments to the Constitution be agreed on by the said Convention—voting by States—and the same be ratified by the Legislatures of two-thirds of the several States, or by conventions in two-thirds thereof—as the one or the other mode of ratification may be proposed by the general convention—they shall thenceforward form a part of this Constitution. But no State shall, without its consent, be deprived of its equal representation in the Senate.

ART. VI

1.—The Government established by this Constitution is the successor of the Provisional Government of the Confederate States of America, and all the laws passed by the latter shall continue in force until the same shall be repealed or modified; and all the officers appointed by the same shall remain in office until their successors are appointed and qualified, or the offices abolished.

2. All debts contracted and engagements entered into before the adoption of this Constitution, shall be as valid against the Confederate States under this Constitution as under the Provisional Government.

3. This Constitution, and the laws of the Confederate States, made in pursuance thereof, and all treaties made, or which shall be made, under the authority of the Confederate States, shall be the supreme law of the land; and the judges in every State shall be bound thereby, any thing in the Constitution or laws of any State to the contrary notwithstanding.

4. The Senators and Representatives before mentioned, and the members of the several State Legislatures, and all executive and judicial officers, both of the Confederate States and of the several States, shall be bound, by oath or affirmation, to support this Constitution; but no re-

ligious test shall ever be required as a qualification to any office or public trust under the Confederate States.

5. The enumeration, in the Constitution, of certain rights, shall not be construed to deny or disparage others retained by the people of the several States.

6. The powers not delegated to the Confederate States by the Constitution, nor prohibited by it to the States, are reserved to the States, respectively, or to the people thereof.

ART. VII

1.—The ratification of the conventions of five States shall be sufficient for the establishment of this Constitution between the States so ratifying the same.

2. When five States shall have ratified this Constitution in the manner before specified, the Congress, under the provisional Constitution, shall prescribe the time for holding the election of President and Vice-President, and for the meeting of the electoral college, and for counting the votes and inaugurating the President. They shall also prescribe the time for holding the first election of members of Congress under this Constitution, and the time for assembling the same. Until the assembling of such Congress, the Congress under the provisional Constitution shall continue to exercise the legislative powers granted them; not extending beyond the time limited by the Constitution of the Provisional Government.

Adopted unanimously by the Congress of the Confederate States of South Carolina, Georgia, Florida, Alabama, Mississippi, Louisiana, and Texas, sitting in convention at the capitol, in the city of Montgomery, Alabama, on the Eleventh day of March, in the year Eighteen Hundred and Sixty-One.

HOWELL COBB
President of the Congress.

(Signatures)

— Document No. 3 —

MESSAGE OF JEFFERSON DAVIS TO THE CONFEDERATE CONGRESS, APRIL 29, 1861 [3]

Lincoln's call for volunteers to aid in putting down "insurrection" in the South amounted to a declaration of war. President Davis immediately sought men for the Confederate Army and asked Congress for powers with which to mobilize land and sea forces and to issue letters of marque and reprisal. By asking authority to receive volunteers, he clearly indicated an intention to bypass requests on the states for militia levies.

⟋   ⟋   ⟋

Gentlemen of the Congress: It is my pleasing duty to announce to you that the Constitution framed for the establishment of a permanent Government for the Confederate States has been ratified by conventions in each of those states to which it was referred. . . . The President of the United States [has] called for an army of 75,000 men. . . . I was not at liberty to disregard the fact that many of the states seemed quite content to submit to the exercise of the power assumed by the President of the United States, and were actively engaged in levying troops. . . . Deprived of the aid of Congress at the moment, I was under the necessity of confining my action to a call on the States for volunteers for the common defense, in accordance with the authority you had confided to me before your adjournment. I deemed it proper, further, to issue [a] proclamation inviting application from persons disposed to aid our defense in private armed vessels on

[3] Dunbar Rowland, ed., *Jefferson Davis, Constitutionalist: His Letters, Papers and Speeches* (10 vols.; Jackson, Miss., 1923), V, 67-84.

the high seas, to the end that preparations might be made
for the immediate issue of letters of marque and reprisal
which you alone, under the Constitution, have power to
grant. . . . I earnestly recommend the immediate passage of a law authorizing me to accept the numerous proposals already received. . . .

There are now in the field at Charleston, Pensacola,
Fort Morgan, Jackson, Saint Philip, and Pulaski 19,000,
and 16,000 are now *en route* for Virginia. It is proposed
to organize and hold in readiness for instant action, in
view of the present exigencies of the country, an army of
100,000 men. If further force should be needed, the wisdom and patriotism of Congress will be confidently appealed to for authority to call into the field additional
numbers of our noble-spirited volunteers who are constantly tendering service far in excess of our wants. . . .

— Document No. 4 —

GENERAL BEAUREGARD ASKS SURRENDER OF FORT SUMTER, APRIL 11, 1861 [4]

*After several weeks of delicate negotiations, weeks of
frustration and dashed hopes, the Confederate government
faced the agonizing question of whether or not it could
permit an enemy fort to exist in Charleston harbor. Political and diplomatic considerations forced the cabinet to
seize Fort Sumter. General Beauregard received orders to
demand surrender of the garrison, and if that were re-*

[4] Jefferson Davis, *Rise and Fall of the Confederate Govern-
    ment* (2 vols.; New York, 1881), I, 285-286.

*fused, to reduce the fort. His communication to Major
Robert Anderson, U.S.A., displays the greatest courtesy.*

Sir: The Government of the Confederate States has
hitherto forborne from any hostile demonstration against
Fort Sumter, in the hope that the Government of the
United States, with a view to the amicable adjustment of
all questions between the two Governments, and to avert
the calamities of war, would voluntarily evacuate it. . . .

But the Confederate States can no longer delay assuming actual possession of a fortification commanding the
entrance of one of their harbors, and necessary to its defense and security.

I am ordered by the Government of the Confederate
States to demand the evacuation of Fort Sumter. . . . All
proper facilities will be afforded for the removal of your-
self and command, together with company arms and property, and all private property, to any post in the United
States which you may elect. The flag which you have upheld so long and with so much fortitude, under the most
trying circumstances, may be saluted by you on taking it
down. . . .

I am, sir, very respectfully, your obedient servant,

G. T. BEAUREGARD,
Brigadier-General commanding.

— Document No. 5 —

MAJOR ANDERSON DECLINES TO SURRENDER SUMTER, APRIL 11, 1861 [5]

Major Robert Anderson, commanding the United States garrison in Fort Sumter, knew he could not hold out indefinitely against Southern attack, especially since he had received no help from the North. He had to reject General Beauregard's demand for surrender, but his reply reflected the cordial atmosphere existing between foemen in Charleston harbor before the Civil War began.

　　　　✓　　　　✓　　　　✓

General: I have the honor to acknowledge the receipt of your communication demanding the evacuation of this fort; and to say in reply thereto that it is a demand with which I regret that my sense of honor and of my obligations to my Government prevents my compliance.

Thanking you for the fair, manly, and courteous terms proposed, and for the high compliment paid me,

I am, General, very respectfully, your obedient servant,

ROBERT ANDERSON,

Major, U. S. Army, commanding.

To Brigadier-General G. T. Beauregard,

Commanding Provisional Army, C. S. A.

[5] Jefferson Davis, *Rise and Fall of the Confederate Government* (2 vols.; New York, 1881), I, 286.

— Document No. 6 —

PROBLEMS OF LIFE IN THE ARMY, OCTOBER 13, 1861[6]

Patriotism and feminine persuasion herded thousands of men into the Confederate ranks early in 1861, but army life lacked virtually all the glories so widely proclaimed. Camps were dreary, monotonous places, filthy, frequently boggy, and always unhealthy. Men soon found that they wasted away from ennui, measles, "flux," and all the timeless ills of armies. With the hard fact of camp life came a wary wisdom, and many Johnny Rebs cautioned friends to spurn the false attraction of glory. The writer of the following letters was a Louisianian from Union Parish, and a brother-in-law of the addressee.

Camp Moore 7 O'clock at night
Oct 13th 1861

J. G. Taylor:

Dr Brother I take the pleasure of writing you a few lines which leaves me enjoying fine health. . . . Jord[an] you spoke as if you had some notion of volunteering. I advise you to stay at home. You could not stand the fair [fare] and hardships of a Soldier. Tell Rufe and Henry to stay at home until I come back, but dont discourage those young men in old Union in any way, for some of them has no sand in their craws no how. . . . I would not take one years wages for what I already have learned about Military affairs. My leaf is full. Write to me often.

E. J. Lee

[6] Frank E. Vandiver, ed., "A Collection of Louisiana Confederate Letters," in the *Louisiana Historical Quarterly*, XXVI (1943), pp. 952-953, 966-968.

Edwards Depot Miss May 20th 1862

Jordan G. Taylor:

It has been so long since I wrote to you that I am almost ashamed to write, but I now have the opportunity and I will make one more faint attempt. I reckon you have heard of our Regt being at Vicksburg, i. e. we are not [at] Vicksburg now, but we are on the R. R. 18 miles from Vicksburg at Edwards Depot. Jord I have been in very bad health ever since Dr Baker left us. I was sick when we left Corinth and was sick all the way. After we got to Vicksburg I stayied [sic] in camps one day and night and had high fever all the time, and could get nothing done for my relief. I then went back to Clinton to the Hospital 10 miles this side of Jackson. There I found the best people I ever saw. My Physician at the Hospital I think was a splendid one, who soon broke my fever and give me a box of pills that has cured my bowels.

I stayed in the Hospital 6 days, and Returned to camps yesterday. I am improving very fast, in fact my health is better now than it has been in two months. The Ladies in Clinton was very kind to me. They visited the Hospital every day, and bring me soup and butter milk and every thing that was nourishing. There is a fine female school there of 70 young Ladies and the prettiest I ever saw. They came to see me every day and would bring me fine bo[u]quets. I tell you I mended fast. . . . Jord I am very anxious to hear from home. I wish you would come to see me. It wont cost you much time nor money. If you cant come write to me and give me all the news. Tell me what the conscript Law is doing among you. I dont want you and Henry [another brother of the writer] to leave home if there is any other chance. I dont see any use of a conscript Law for the South cant arm the men that's now out. . . . Give my Respects to all enquiring friends.

Write to me at Edwards Depot, Hindes County Miss. Adieu

E. J. LEE

Camp Ouachita Near Vicksburg Dec 7th 1862

J. G. Taylor:

Sir I seat myself this sabbath evening to write you [a] few lines, which leaves me in tol[e]rable health. I wrote to Mother the day after I got here, but you may get this before she gets hers as I will send this to Monroe by hand. I stood my trip well, though I had a muddy time of it. I was mustered into service yesterday morning by Lt Col M. Rogers. . . . Bro Henry is sick at this time with Jaundice. The 31st Regt is very sickly, for the last three nights they have lost Seven men out of the Regt. Our Regt is in better health than it ever was, our boys looks healthy, and are in fine spirits. Our Regt is well drilled and dissiplened [*sic*]. The we[a]ther is fair and cold. The 31st Regt are not in fine spirits, those that are not down sick are greiving [*sic*] themselves to death about home. I want you to send my shoes to me by the first chance. As you have nothing to do untill [*sic*] a new year you had as well come and b[r]ing me some meat. We dont get any thing to eat but corn bread and beef. The boys say that they have not had any flour or coffee since I left so you know it is hard liveing [*sic*]. Our beef is old and very lean, we Just have to boil it and it dont make any sop. Steve Beard and Leander McFarland has written home for some hog meat, and we want you to put it all in a box and bring it to us. . . .

Yours Respectfully,
E. J. Lee

— Document No. 7 —

FIRST CONFEDERATE CONSCRIPTION LAW, APRIL 16, 1862[7]

In April, 1862, the Confederate Government recognized the dangerous possibility that without some form of

[7] James M. Matthews, ed., *Statutes at Large of the Confederate States of America* (Richmond, 1862), I Congress, 1 Session, chapter XXXI.

*force, the Southern armies would melt away. The first
contingents of twelve-months volunteers approached the
end of their enlistment term and talked loudly of going
home; recruiting had slacked off with alarming speed.
Regiments already organized had to be retained, new ones
mobilized. The only solution was conscription, and the
Confederate Congress passed the first general draft law in
American history.*

✓   ✓   ✓

An Act to Further Provide for the Public Defence

In view of the exigencies of the country, and the absolute necessity of keeping in the service our gallant army,
and of placing in the field a large additional force to meet
the advancing columns of the enemy now invading our
soil: Therefore

*The Congress of the Confederate States of America do
enact,* That the President be, and he is hereby authorized
to call out and place in the military service of the Confederate States, for three years, unless the war shall have
been sooner ended, all white men who are residents of
the Confederate States, between the ages of eighteen and
thirty-five years at the time the call or calls may be made,
who are not legally exempted from military service. All
of the persons aforesaid who are now in the armies of the
Confederacy, and whose term of service will expire before
the end of the war, shall be continued in the service for
three years from the date of their original enlistment. . . .

Provided, however, That all such companies, squadrons,
battalions, and regiments, whose term of original enlistment was for twelve months, shall have the right, within
forty days, on a day to be fixed by the Commander of the
Brigade, to re-organize said companies, battalions, and
regiments, by electing all their officers, which they had a
right heretofore to elect, who shall be commissioned by
the President: *Provided, further,* That furloughs not exceeding sixty days, with transportation home and back,
shall be granted to all those retained in the service by the
provisions of this Act beyond the period of their original
enlistment, and who have not heretofore received furloughs. . . . *Provided, further,* That in lieu of a furlough

the commutation value in money of the transportation herein above granted, shall be paid to each private, musician, or non-commissioned officer who may elect to receive it, at such time as the furlough would otherwise be granted: *Provided, further,* That all persons under the age of eighteen years or over the age of thirty-five years, who are now enrolled in the military service of the Confederate States, in the regiments, squadrons, battalions, and companies hereafter to be reorganized, shall be required to remain in their respective companies, squadrons, battalions and regiments for ninety days, unless their places can be sooner supplied by other recruits not now in service, who are between the ages of eighteen and thirty-five years; and all laws and parts of laws providing for the re-enlistment of volunteers and the organization thereof into companies, squadrons, battalions, or regiments, shall be and the same are hereby repealed. . . .

SEC. 3. *Be it further enacted,* That for the enrollment of all persons comprehended within the provisions of this Act, who are not already in service in the armies of the Confederate States, it shall be lawful for the President, with the consent of the Governors of the respective States, to employ State officers, and on failure to obtain such consent, he shall employ Confederate officers, charged with the duty of making such enrollment in accordance with rules and regulations to be prescribed by him.

SEC. 4. *Be it further enacted,* That persons enrolled under the provisions of the preceding Section, shall be assigned by the Secretary of War, to the different companies now in the service, until each company is filled to its maximum number, and the persons so enrolled shall be assigned to companies from the States from which they respectively come.

SEC. 5. *Be it further enacted,* That all Seamen and ordinary Seamen in the land forces of the Confederate States, enrolled under the provisions of this Act, may, on application of the Secretary of the Navy, be transferred from the land forces to the Naval service.

SEC. 6. *Be it further enacted,* That in all cases where a State may not have in the army a number of Regiments, Battalions, Squadrons or Companies, sufficient to absorb the number of persons subject to military service under this Act, belonging to such State, then the residue or excess thereof, shall be kept as a reserve, under such regulations as may be established by the Secretary of War, and that at stated periods of not greater than three months, details, determined by lot, shall be made from said reserve, so that each company shall, as nearly as practicable, be kept full: *Provided,* That the persons held in reserve may remain at home until called into service by the President: *Provided, also,* That during their stay at home, they shall not receive pay: *Provided, further,* That the persons comprehended in this Act, shall not be subject to the Rules and Articles of War, until mustered into the actual service of the Confederate States; except that said persons, when enrolled and liable to duty, if they shall wilfully refuse to obey said call, each of them shall be held to be a deserter, and punished as such, under said Articles: *Provided, further,* That whenever, in the opinion of the President, the exigencies of the public service may require it, he shall be authorized to call into actual service the entire reserve, or so much as may be necessary, not previously assigned to different companies in service under provision of section four of this Act; said reserve shall be organized under such rules as the Secretary of War may adopt: *Provided,* The company, battalion and regimental officers shall be elected by the troops composing the same: *Provided,* The troops raised in any one State shall not be combined in regimental, battalion, squadron or company organization with troops raised in any other States.

Sec. 7. *Be it further enacted,* That all soldiers now serving in the army or mustered in the military service of the Confederate States, or enrolled in said service under the authorizations heretofore issued by the Secretary of War, and who are continued in the service by virtue of this Act, who have not received the bounty of fifty dollars allowed by existing laws, shall be entitled to receive said bounty.

Sec. 8. *Be it further enacted,* That each man who may hereafter be mustered into service, and who shall arm himself with a musket, shot-gun, rifle or carbine, accepted as an efficient weapon, shall be paid the value thereof, to be ascertained by the mustering officer under such regulations as may be prescribed by the Secretary of War, if he is willing to sell the same, and if he is not, then he shall be entitled to receive one dollar a month for the use of said received and approved musket, rifle, shot-gun or carbine.

SEC. 9. *Be it further enacted,* That persons not liable for duty may be received as substitutes for those who are, under such regulations as may be prescribed by the Secretary of War.

SEC. 10. *Be it further enacted,* That all vacancies shall be filled by the President from the company, battalion, squadron or regiment in which such vacancies shall occur, by promotion according to seniority, except in case of disability or other incompetency: *Provided, however,* That the President may, when in his opinion, it may be proper, fill such vacancy or vacancies by the promotion of any officer or officers, or private or privates from such company, battalion, squadron or regiment who shall have been distinguished in the service by exhibition of valor and skill; and that whenever a vacancy shall occur in the lowest grade of the commissioned officers of a company, said vacancy shall be filled by election: *Provided,* That all appointments made by the President shall be by and with the advice and consent of the Senate.

SEC. 11. *Be it further enacted,* That the provisions of the first section of this Act, relating to the election of officers, shall apply to those regiments, battalions, and squadrons which are composed of twelve months and war companies combined in the same organization, without regard to the manner in which the officers thereof were originally appointed.

SEC. 12. *Be it further enacted,* That each company of infantry shall consist of one hundred and twenty-five, rank and file; each company of field artillery of one hundred and fifty, rank and file; each of cavalry, of eighty, rank and file.

SEC. 13. *Be it further enacted,* That all persons, subject to enrollment, who are not now in the service, under the provisions of this Act, shall be permitted, previous to such enrollment, to volunteer in companies now in the service.

Approved April 16, 1862.

— Document No. 8 —

DAVIS ON CONSCRIPTION AND EXEMPTION, DECEMBER 7, 1863[8]

As the Confederate War Department gained experience enforcing the draft law of April, 1862, it became clear that the cumbersome practices of substitution and exemption offered large loopholes for draft evaders. President Davis sought authority to plug these loopholes by enrolling all eligible men and then detailing some for essential war work. But Congress never seemed to approve of this system; apparently it concentrated too much power in the hands of the President. Davis' reasons for wanting this power follow.

✓   ✓   ✓

Richmond, Va.

To the Senate and House of Representatives of the Confederate States.

. . . In view of the large conscription recently ordered by the enemy and their subsequent call for volunteers, to be followed if ineffectual by a still further draft, we are admonished that no effort must be spared to add largely to our effective force as promptly as possible. The sources of supply are to be found by restoring to the Army all who are improperly absent, putting an end to substitution, modifying the exemption law, restricting details, and placing in the ranks such of the able-bodied men now employed as wagoners, nurses, cooks, and other employees as are doing service for which the negroes may be found competent.

The act of 16th of April, 1862, provides "that persons not liable for duty may be received as substitutes for those who are, under such regulations as may be pre-

[8] Dunbar Rowland, ed., *Jefferson Davis, Constitutionalist. His Letters, Papers, and Speeches* (10 vols.; Jackson, Miss., 1923), VI, 117-118.

scribed by the Secretary of War." The policy of granting this privilege has not been sustained by experience. Not only has the numerical strength of the Army been seriously impaired by the frequent desertions for which substitutes have become notorious, but dissatisfaction has been excited among those who have been unable or unwilling to avail themselves of the opportunity thus afforded of avoiding the military service of their country.

I fully concur in the opinion expressed by the Secretary [of War] that there is no ground for the objection that a new provision to include those who furnished substitutes under the former call would be a breach of contract. To accept a substitute was to confer a privilege, not to enter into a contract, and whenever the substitute is rendered liable to conscription, it would seem to follow that the principal, whose place he had taken, should respond for him, as the Government had received no consideration for his exemption. . . .

On the subject of exemptions, it is believed that abuses cannot be checked unless the system is placed on a basis entirely different from that now provided by law. The object of your legislation has been not to confer privileges on classes, but to exonerate from military duty such number of persons skilled in the various trades, professions, and mechanical pursuits as could render more valuable service to their country by laboring in their present occupation than by going into the ranks of the Army. The policy is unquestionable, but the result would, it is thought, be better obtained by enrolling all such persons and allowing details to be made of the number necessary to meet the wants of the country. Considerable numbers are believed to be now exempted from the military service who are not needful to the public in their civil vocation.

Certain duties are now performed throughout the country by details from the Army which could be as well executed by persons above the present conscript age. An extension of the limit so as to embrace persons over forty-five years and physically fit for service in guarding posts, railroads, and bridges, in apprehending deserters, and, where practicable, assuming the place of younger men detailed for duty with the Niter, Ordnance, Commissary, and Quartermaster's Bureaus of the War Department, would, it is hoped, add largely to the effective force in the field without an undue burden on the population.

If to the above measures be added a law to enlarge the policy of the act of the 21st of April, 1862, so as to enable the Department to replace not only enlisted cooks, but wagoners and other employees in the Army, by negroes, it is hoped that the ranks of the Army will be so strengthened for the ensuing campaign as to put to defiance the utmost efforts of the enemy. . . .

— Document No. 9 —

ENROLLMENT OF SLAVES IN THE ARMY, MARCH 13, 1865[9]

As early as 1863 some high ranking army officers urged the Confederate government to use slaves as soldiers. The suggestion, regarded as almost treasonable, was forgotten, but the Administration did go so far as to ask that slaves be used for housekeeping duties in the armies—hospital stewards, ambulance drivers, cooks, teamsters. Congress approved. And when desperation came with attrition, Southern lawmakers finally authorized putting slaves in the ranks as soldiers. In the law covering Negro enrollment, careful attention was given to the master-slave relationship.

↗   ↗   ↗

[9] *War of the Rebellion: A Compilation of the Official Records of the Union and Confederate Armies* (127 vols. and index; Washington, 1880-1901), Series IV, vol. 3, p. 1161.

An Act to Increase the Military force of the Confederate States

The Congress of the Confederate States of America do enact, That in order to provide additional forces to repel invasion, maintain the rightful possession of the Confederate States, secure their independence, and preserve their institutions, the President be, and he is hereby, authorized to ask for and accept from the owners of slaves, the services of such number of able-bodied negro men as he may deem expedient, for and during the war, to perform military service in whatever capacity he may direct.

Sec. 2. That the General-in-Chief be authorized to organize the said slaves into companies, battalions, regiments and brigades, under such rules and regulations as the Secretary of War may prescribe, and to be commanded by such officers as the President may appoint.

Sec. 3. That while employed in the service the said troops shall receive the same rations, clothing and compensation as are allowed to other troops in the same branch of the service.

Sec. 4. That if, under the previous sections of this act, the President shall not be able to raise a sufficient number of troops to prosecute the war successfully and maintain the sovereignty of the States and the independence of the Confederate States, then he is hereby authorized to call on each State, whenever he thinks it expedient, for her quota of 300,000 troops, in addition to those subject to military service under existing laws, or so many thereof as the President may deem necessary for the purposes herein mentioned, to be raised from such classes of the population, irrespective of color, in each State, as the proper authorities thereof may determine: *Provided,* that not more than twenty-five per cent of the male slaves between the ages of eighteen and forty-five, in any State, shall be called for under the provisions of this act.

Sec. 5. That nothing in this act shall be construed to authorize a change in the relation which the said slaves shall bear toward their owners, except by consent of the owners and of the States in which they may reside, and in pursuance of the laws thereof.

Approved, March 13, 1865.

— Document No. 10 —

ACT REGULATING IMPRESSMENTS, MARCH 26, 1863[10]

Confederate Army and Navy supply officers wrestled continuously with the problem of obtaining food, clothing, transportation, munitions. As money declined in value and prices rose, it became necessary to commandeer private property for military use. Impressment, one of the most hated of government policies, began early in the war and came under legal regulation in 1863.

✓   ✓   ✓

AN ACT TO REGULATE IMPRESSMENTS

The Congress of the Confederate States of America do enact, That whenever the exigencies of any army in the field are such as to make impressments of forage, articles of subsistence or other property absolutely necessary, then such impressments may be made by the officer or officers whose duty it is to furnish such forage, articles of subsistence or other property for such army. In cases where the owner of such property and the impressing officer cannot agree upon the value thereof, it shall be the duty of such impressing officer, upon an affidavit in writing of the owner of such property, or his agent, that such property was grown, raised or produced by said owner, or is held or has been purchased by him, not for sale or speculation, but for his own use or consumption, to cause the same to be ascertained and determine by the judgment of two loyal and disinterested citizens of the city, county or parish in

[10] James M. Matthews, ed., *Statutes at Large of the Confederate States of America* (Richmond, 1863), I Congress, 3 Session, chapter X.

which such impressments may be made; one to be selected by the owner; one by the impressing officer; and in the event of their disagreement, these two shall choose an umpire of like qualifications, whose decision shall be final. The persons thus selected, after an oath to appraise the property impressed, fairly and impartially . . . shall proceed to assess just compensation for the property so impressed, whether the absolute ownership, or the temporary use thereof, only is required.

SEC. 2. That the officer or person impressing property, as aforesaid, shall, at the time of said taking, pay to the owner, his agent or attorney, the compensation fixed by said appraisers; and shall also give to the owner, or person controlling said property, a certificate, over his official signature, specifying the battalion, regiment, brigade, division or corps to which he belongs; that said property is essential for the use of the army, could not be otherwise procured, and was taken through absolute necessity. . . . Said certificate shall be evidence for the owner, as well of the taking of said property for the public use, as the right of the owner to the amount of compensation fixed as aforesaid. And in case said officer or person taking said property shall have failed to pay the owner or his agent, said compensation as hereinbefore required, then said owner shall be entitled to the speedy payment of the same by the proper disbursing officer; which, when so paid, shall be in full satisfaction of all claims against the government of the Confederate States.

SEC. 3. Whenever the appraisement provided for in the first section of this act, shall, for any reason, be impracticable at the time of said impressment, then and in that case the value of the property impressed shall be assessed as soon as possible, by two loyal and disinterested citizens of the city, county, or parish, wherein the property was taken. . . .

SEC. 4. That whenever the Secretary of War shall be of opinion that it is necessary to take private property for public use, by reason of the impracticability of procuring the same by purchase, so as to accumulate necessary supplies for the army, or the good of the service, in any locality, he may, by general order, through the proper subordinate officers, authorize such property to be taken for the public use; the compensation due the owner for the same to be determined, and the value fixed as provided for in the first and second sections of this act.

SEC. 5. That it shall be the duty of the President, as early as practicable after the passage of this act, to appoint a commissioner in each State where property shall be taken for the public use, and request the Governor of such of the States in which the President shall appoint said commissioner, to appoint another commissioner, to act in conjunction with the commissioner appointed by the President, who shall receive the compensation or [of] eight dollars per day, and ten cents per mile as mileage, to be paid by the Confederate Government. Said commissioners shall constitute a board, whose duty it shall be to fix upon the prices to be paid by the government, for all property impressed or taken for the public use as aforesaid, so as to afford just compensation to the owners thereof. Said commissioners shall agree upon and publish a schedule of prices every two months, or oftner [sic] if they shall deem it proper; and in the event they shall not be able to agree in any matter confided to them in this act, they shall have power to appoint an umpire to decide the matter in dispute, whose decision shall be the decision of the board; and said umpire shall receive the same rate of compensation for the time he shall serve, allowed to said commissioners respectively: *Provided,* That said commissioners shall be residents of the State for which they shall be appointed; and if the Governor of any State shall refuse or neglect to appoint said commissioner within ten days after a request to do so by the President, then the President shall appoint both commissioners, by and with the advice and consent of the Senate.

SEC. 6. That all property impressed or taken for the public use, as aforesaid, in the hands of any person other than the persons who have raised, grown or produced the same, or persons holding the same for their own use or consumption, and who shall make the affidavit as hereinbefore required, shall be paid for according to the schedule of prices fixed by the commissioners as aforesaid. But if the officer impressing or taking for the public use such property, and the owner shall differ as to the quality of the article or property impressed or taken, as aforesaid, thereby making it fall within a higher or lower price named in the schedule, then the owner or agent, and the officer impressing or taking, as aforesaid, may select each a loyal and disinterested citizen . . . to determine the quality of said article or property, who shall, in case of disagreement, appoint an umpire of like qualifications, and his decision, if approved by the officer impressing, shall be final; but if not approved, the impressing officer shall send the award to the commissioners of the State where the property is impressed, with his reasons for disapproving the same, and said commissioners may hear such proofs as the parties may respectively adduce, and their decision shall be final: *Provided,* That the owner may receive the price offered by the impressing officer, without prejudice to his claim to receive the higher compensation.

SEC. 7. That the property necessary for the support of the owner and his family, and to carry on his ordinary agricultural and mechanical business, to be ascertained by the appraisers, to be appointed as provided in the first section of this act, under oath, shall not be taken or impressed for the public use; and when the impressing officer and the owner cannot agree as to the quantity necessary, as aforesaid, then the decision of the said appraisers shall be binding on the officer and all other persons.

SEC. 8. Where property has been impressed for temporary use, and is lost or destroyed without the default of the owner, the Government of the Confederate States shall pay a just compensation therefor; to be ascertained by appraisers appointed and qualified as provided in the first section of this act. If such property when returned has, in the opinion of the owner, been injured whilst in the public use, the amount of damage thereby sustained, shall be determined in the manner described in the third section of this act, the officer returning the property being authorized to act on behalf of the government; and upon such inquiry, the certificate of the value of the property, when originally impressed, shall be received as *prima facie* evidence of the value thereof.

SEC. 9. Where slaves are impressed by the Confederate Government to labor on fortifications or other public works, the impressment shall be made by said government according to the rules and regulations provided in the laws of the State wherein they are impressed; and in the absence of such law, in accordance with such rules and regulations not inconsistent with the provisions of this act, as the Secretary of War shall from time to time prescribe: *Provided,* That no impressment of slaves shall be made when they can be hired or procured by the consent of the owner or agent.

Sec. 10. That previous to the first day of December next, no slave laboring on a farm or plantation, exclusively devoted to the production of grain and provisions, shall be taken for the public use without the consent of the owner, except in case of urgent necessity.

Sec. 11. That any commissioned or non-commissioned officer or private who shall violate the provisions of this act, shall be tried before the military court of the corps to which he is attached, on complaint made by the owner or other person, and on conviction, if an officer, he shall be cashiered and put into the ranks as a private; and if a non-commissioned officer or private, he shall suffer such punishment, not inconsistent with military law, as the court may direct.

Approved March 26, 1863.

— Document No. 11 —

GOVERNMENT PRICE SCHEDULE, SEPTEMBER 15, 1863[11]

Under the "Act to Regulate Impressments," commissioners were appointed in various states to establish fair prices for commodities. Schedules published by the appraisers were guides to government impressing officers and at the same time constituted a Confederate attempt at voluntary price fixing. The following table gives the prices set by the commissioners in South Carolina. It indicates the wide variety of things which came under impressment.

[11] *Official Records of the Union and Confederate Armies,* Series IV, vol. 2, pp. 836-837.

The open market price of all items was usually several times higher.

✔   ✔   ✔

Apples, dried, good quality, peeled, per bushel 28 lbs.	$ 3.00
Apples, dried, good quality, unpeeled, per bushel	2.00
Axes, good quality, with handles, each . .	5.00
Bacon, good quality, sides, per pound . . .	.75
Bacon, good quality, hams, per pound . . .	.70
Bacon, good quality, shoulders, per pound . .	.65
Bacon, good quality, jowls, per pound . . .	.40
Beans, good quality, white or corn-field, per bushel	3.00
Brandy, good quality, apple, per gallon . . .	4.00
Beef, good quality, fresh, per pound . . .	.25
Beef, good quality, salt or corned, per pound .	.50
Beef, good quality, cattle, per pound . . .	.18
Candles, good quality, tallow, per pound . .	1.00
Chains, good quality, trace, per pair . . .	2.50
Cloth, good quality, woolen, for soldiers' clothes, ¾ yard wide, 10 ounces to yard, and pro rata as to greater or less weight or width. Per yard	4.00
Coffee, good quality, Rio, per pound . . .	3.00
Corn, good quality, unshelled, per bushel of 70 lbs.	1.95
Corn, good quality, shelled, sacks not included, per bushel of 56 lbs.	2.00
Cornmeal, good quality, sacks not included, per bushel of 50 lbs.	2.00
Drills, good quality, cotton, ⅞ yard wide, 3 yards to pound, per yard	.65
Flour, good quality, extra family, per barrel of 196 lbs.	22.00
Flour, good quality, extra family, per sack of 98 lbs.	11.00
Flour, good quality, superfine, per barrel of 196 lbs.	20.00
Flour, good quality, superfine, per sack of 98 lbs.	10.00

Flour, good quality, fine, per barrel of 196 lbs.	18.00
Flour, good quality, fine, per sack of 98 lbs	9.00
Fodder, good quality, baled, per 100 lbs.	2.50
Hats, good quality, wool, each	3.25
Hay, good quality, baled, per 100 lbs.	1.50
Hogs, good quality, per pound	1.25
Hides, good quality, dry, per pound	1.25
Hides, good quality, green, per pound	.50
Horses, good quality, artillery, first class, per head	500.00
Horses, good quality, artillery, second class, per head	400.00
Iron, good quality, pig, per ton of 2,240 lbs.	85.00
Iron, good quality, square or round, per ton	350.00
Iron, good quality, flat or band, per ton	320.00
Iron, good quality, hoop, per ton	440.00
Iron, good quality, boiler plate, per ton	500.00
Iron, good quality, serviceable railroad, per ton	175.00
Iron, good quality, unserviceable railroad, per ton	75.00
Jeans, good quality, wool, domestic, per yard	4.00
Kettles, good quality, camp, iron, each	5.00
Lard, good quality, clean, per pound	.75
Leather, good quality, sole, per pound	2.50
Leather, good quality, upper, per pound	3.25
Leather, good quality, harness, per pound	3.00
Molasses, good quality, cane, per gallon	5.00
Molasses, good quality, sorghum, per gallon	3.00
Mules, good quality, first class, per head	400.00
Mules, good quality, second class, per head	350.00
Mules, good quality, third class, per head	250.00
Oats, good quality, sheaf, unbaled, per 100 lbs.	2.00
Oats, good quality, sheaf, baled, per 100 lbs.	2.50
Osnaburgs, good quality, cotton, ¾ yard wide, 7 ounces to yard, per yard	.60
Osnaburgs, good quality, cotton, ⅞ yard wide, 8 ounces to yard, per yard	.70
Peas, good quality, cow, per bushel of 60 lbs	2.00
Potatoes, good quality, Irish, per bushel of 60 lbs.	2.00
Potatoes, good quality, sweet, per bushel of 60 lbs.	1.00

Peaches, good quality, dried, peeled, per bushel
of 38 lbs. 5.00
Pork, good quality, fresh, per pound 35
Pork, good quality, salt, per pound 55
Pasturage, good quality, cattle and horses near
city, per head per month 3.00
Pasturage, good quality, interior, per head per
month 1.50
Rice, good quality, new, per pound 15
Rice, good quality, old, per pound 12
Sacks, good quality, two bushels, osnaburg,
each 1.00
Shirting, good quality, cotton, ¾ yard wide,
4½ yards to pound, per yard 50
Shirting, good quality, cotton, ⅞ yard wide,
3¾ yards to pound, per yard 60
Salt, good quality, coast, per bushel of 50
lbs. 15.00
Salt, good quality, Liverpool, per bushel of 50
lbs. 30.00
Shoes, good quality, army, per pair . . . 8.00
Shoe thread, good quality, flax, per pound . . 3.00
Socks, good quality, soldiers' wool, per pair . 1.25
Sheep, good quality, fat, per head 15.00
Sugar, good quality, brown, common, per
pound 90
Soap, good quality, hard, per pound 40
Soap, good quality, soft, per pound 20
Tea, good quality, black, per pound . . . 5.00
Tea, good quality, green, per pound . . . 7.00
Tent cloth, good quality, cotton, 10 ounces to
yard, per yard 90
Vinegar, good quality, cider, per gallon . . 1.00
Vinegar, good quality, manufactured, per gal-
lon 75
Whisky, good quality, good, per gallon . . 4.00
Wheat, good quality, first rate, white, per bushel
of 60 lbs. 4.00
Wagons, good quality, wood axle, 4-horse, new,
each 250.00
Wagons, good quality, iron axle, 4-horse, new . 300.00

— Document No. 12 —

MAKESHIFT MEDICINES AND SUBSTITUTE RECIPES, 1863 [12]

With medicines in short supply and all sorts of commodities scarce, the Surgeon-General's Office assigned Francis P. Porcher, South Carolinian, the task of preparing a Confederate herbal which would inform the public of the special properties in various Southern flora. The book he published, Resources of the Southern Fields and Forests *(1863), is still good reading. During the war it filled a vital need; the excerpts given below show the wide scope of Porcher's work.*

✓   ✓   ✓

MAIZE—INDIAN CORN.

A Substitute for Coffee was recommended as follows during the period of scarcity: For a family of seven or eight persons, take a pint of well toasted corn meal and add to it as much water as an ordinary sized coffee pot will hold, and then boil it well. We have tried this toasted meal coffee, and prefer it. Many persons cannot drink coffee with impunity, and we advise all such to try the receipt. They will find it more nutritious than coffee, and quite as palatable. . . .

Oil of a fine quality is manufactured from corn. 'It is said to burn with a clear, steady light, in every respect equal to sperm or lard oil, without the smoke which usually attends vegetable oils, and will not congeal in the coldest weather.' A liquor, well known as Corn Whiskey, is also distilled from the fermented grain.

[12] Francis Peyre Porcher, *Resources of the Southern Fields and Forests* (Charleston, 1869). The selection dealing with Maize appears on p. 636; the selection dealing with White Rush, on pp. 678-679; the selection dealing with Dandelion on pp. 471-473.

WHITE RUSH; RUSH-LIKE SPARTINA, (*Spartina juncea, . . . Limnetis. . . .*) Grows in the salt water marshes; vicinity of Charleston; often immersed. . . .

The flowers are purgative. The oil from the young branches is caustic, and is employed against ring-worm, and in cutaneous eruptions generally. The leaves are pungent. 'It has been proposed as a cultivated field plant for yielding fibre, and it would produce well on poor, salicious soils, which are unfit for flax or corn. Its manufactured fibre is clear, and as strong and soft as that of flax, but is deficient in length. The plant is of small value for forage.'

DANDELION, (*Taraxacum dens-leonis. . . .*) I have observed it growing in the streets of Charleston and New York; Newbern. . . .

The root is deobstruent, cathartic and diuretic. 'Good in obstructions of the viscera, scirrhosites of the liver, stone in the gall-bladder, ascites, jaundice,' etc. A decoction of the root is also useful in impetigo and itch; the doses are one drachm of the juice and two ounces of the decoction. . . . At Gottingen the roots are washed and substituted for *coffee* by the poorer inhabitants; they say the difference between this and the imported article can scarcely be distinguished. It is roasted, powdered and prepared in the same manner. . . .

Dr. Wood, in the U. S. Disp., says that his experience in derangements of the biliary secretions has been decidedly in its favor, it being particularly valuable in chronic hepatitis. Eberle recommends it in chronic cases of infantile jaundice. Griffith . . . alludes to its use in deranged conditions of the digestive organs, connected with an abnormal state of the liver, and in dropsical effusions arising from the same cause. . . . It has been employed, likewise, in affections of the spleen, uterine obstructions, chronic cutaneous disorders, etc. When its diuretic effect is desired, it is advised that it be given in combination with supertartrate of potash. . . .

The young shoots are edible, and produce in children a diuretic effect. . . . I have given the extract largely during many years attendance at the Marine and City Hospitals, Charleston. I ascertain that it certainly produces a laxative effect given in from ten to thirty grains—the same, or a much larger quantity dissolved in water, proved diuretic. In this way I account for the different qualities ascribed to it. There was always a tendency to ascribe a power in the dandelion to act upon the portal system. . . . It is a useful vegetable laxative in place of calomel.

— Document No. 13 —

"OUR MARTYRS" BY P. H. HAYNE[13]

Southern war poetry ranged usually from maudlin to doggerel, but a few Confederate poets did excellent work. Among the best were Henry Timrod and Paul Hamilton Hayne. Hayne had devoted his prewar career to writing and earned a sound reputation in South Carolina literary circles. War touched him deeply and generated some of his finest verse. "Our Martyrs" gained wide attention, and ranked as a superior war poem.

I am sitting alone and weary,   3
  By the hearth of my darkened room,
And the low wind's *miserere*,
  Makes sadder the midnight gloom.
"There's a nameless terror nigh me—
  There's a phantom spell on the air,
And methinks, that the dead glide by me,
  And the breath of the grave's in my hair!"

'Tis a vision of ghastly faces,
  All pallid and worn with pain,
Where the splendor of manful graces
  Shines dim thro' a scarlet rain:—

[13] *Poems of Paul Hamilton Hayne, Complete Edition, With Numerous Illustrations* (Boston, 1882), pp. 85-86.

In a wild and weird procession
   They sweep by my startled eyes,
And stern with their Fate's fruition,
   Seem melting in blood-red skies. . . .

Alas! for our heroes perished!
   Cut down at their golden prime,
With the luminous hopes they cherished,
   On the height of their faith sublime!
For them is the voice of wailing
   And the sweet blush-rose departs.
From the cheeks of the maidens paling
   O'er the wreck of their broken hearts.

And alas! for the vanished glory
   Of a thousand household spells!
And alas! for the tearful story
   Of the spirit's fond farewells!
By the flood, on the field, in the forest,
   Our bravest have yielded breath,
Yet the shafts that have smitten the sorest,
   Were launched by a viewless death.

Oh, Thou! that hast charms of healing,
   Descend on a widowed land,
And bind o'er the wounds of feeling,
   The balms of thy mystic hand;
Till the lives that lament and languish,
   Renewed by a touch divine,
From the depths of their mortal anguish
   May rise to the calm of Thine.

— Document No. 14 —

A PROPOSED COMMERCIAL TREATY, APRIL 18, 1862 [14]

Faced with a crisis in King Cotton diplomacy in 1862, Davis' administration wrestled with the problem of coercing Europe into recognition of Southern independence. The Confederate Senate proposed to the President that Europe be offered certain cotton and trade concessions. The following resolution reflects lingering Rebel optimism.

↑   ↑   ↑

Resolved by the Senate of the Confederate States of America, That the President is hereby respectfully requested to instruct the commissioners from this Government to Her Britannic Majesty, His Imperial Majesty the Emperor of the French, and Her Majesty the Queen of Spain, to propose to them the following terms for a treaty of amity and commerce between the said Governments and the Government of the Confederate States:

First. That the Governments of Great Britain, France, and Spain shall declare the inefficiency and consequent illegality of the blockade of the ports in the Confederate States by the Government of the United States, and that they maintain in our waters during the war with the United States a sufficient number of war vessels, in connection with the navy of the Confederate States, to enforce the declaration and effectually raise the blockade.

Second. That the Governments of Great Britain, France, and Spain shall supply and transport to the Confederate Government such arms, ammunition, and munitions of war as may be needed in the prosecution of the war with the United States, the Government of the Confederate States paying therefor the market value of the

[14] *Official Records of the Union and Confederate Armies,* Series IV, vol. 1, p. 1073.

articles so furnished; and that in any treaty of peace hereafter to be entered into between the Confederate States
and the United States the decision of all questions in said
treaty in regard to boundaries shall be under the sole and
exclusive judgment and control of the Confederate States.

Third. That the President be authorized to offer to the
Governments of Great Britain, France, and Spain such
discriminations in favor of British, French, and Spanish
commerce and navigation, foreign and coastwise, as he
may find to be necessary to secure the aid and co-opera-
tion of the British, French, and Spanish Governments for
the purposes aforesaid, and which shall be in accordance
with the true interests of the Confederate States.

Fourth. The treaty, when made according to the foregoing terms, to continue of force for _____ years,
after which time either party may annul the same, having
given twelve months' notice of such intention.

Agreed to by the Senate of the Confederate States of
America, April 18, 1862.

JAMES H. NASH,
Secretary

— Document No. 15 —

MEDIATION CONSIDERED BY ENGLAND, SEPTEMBER-OCTOBER, 1862 [15]

*As Confederate fortunes improved through the late
summer and early fall of 1862, British interest in recognition rose. When Lee's army pushed invaders out of Vir-*

[15] All of the Palmerston letters are from the Lord Palmerston
Papers, Broadlands, England. They are made available
through the courtesy of Earl Mountbatten of Burma.

ginia and stood poised for an advance into Maryland, Lord John Russell reached the conclusion that mediation and recognition were necessary. Lord Palmerston was not quite persuaded, but the cabinet was alerted to a discussion of these vital questions and Southern diplomacy balanced on the edge of success. The several letters printed below indicate the shifting opinions of the British government.

✓   ✓   ✓

Gotha, September 17, 1862

My dear Palmerston,

Whether the Federal Army is destroyed or not it is clear that it is driven back to Washington, and has made no progress in subduing the Insurgent States.

Such being the case, I agree with you that the time is come for offering Mediation to the United States Government, with a view of the recognition of the Independence of the Confederates.— I agree farther that in case of failure, we ought ourselves to recognise the Southern States, as an Independent State.—

For the purpose of taking so important a step, I think we must have a Meeting of the Cabinet, the 23rd or the 30th would suit me for the Meeting.—

We ought then, if we agree on such a step, to propose it first to France, and then on the part of England and France to Russia and other Powers as a Measure decided upon by us.—

We ought I think in proposing Mediation to the U. S. to repeat our declaration of Neutrality.—

We ought to make ourselves safe in Canada, not by sending more troops there, but by concentrating those we have in a few defensible points, before the Winter sets in. . . .

Yours truly,
RUSSELL.

Gotha, September 29, 1862

My dear Lord John,

. . . Meade has given me your message—viz: that the Cabinet is likely to be summoned to consider the present state of the American Question. Whether the time is not come to offer Mediation of H[er] M[ajesty]'s Government, and in case of refusal to recognise the Southern

Confederacy.— When I last saw Lord Palmerston he mentioned the subject to me, so that I have had time to think it over.—

If we were asked to Mediate we could not refuse.— The North hate us now— The Southern Leaders did hate us and may for all we know do so now, or hereafter.

And therefore we might selfishly argue that it was not politically disadvantageous to us that both parties should exhaust themselves a little more before they make Peace.— It would however be Monstrous not to avail ourselves of a good opportunity to put an End to the Crimes and Calamities which are now desolating North America and inflicting at the same time injury on our Commerce and Manufactures. But the difficulties of Mediation are great.— Public opinion in England is diametrically opposed to that of both Northern and Southern Statesmen on Slavery.— The questions of boundary are of vital importance, not only to the North and South, but to the West.— The negotiations would have to be carried on in connexion with the French, who altho' they want Cotton, are partial to the North.— I doubt whether any European Government really understands American Politics, or the objects of the North and of the South, and of the different States once released from the hope of preserving the great Union, or the views of the different important Parties in the Republic.—

I doubt whether in offering to Mediate, we should do so with any bona-fide Expectation of its being accepted.— If either or both Parties wished for Mediation we should certainly have had some (more or less direct) intimation of it.—

It is possible that one or both Belligerents might accept the offer of Mediation, not with a view to Peace, or with the intention of making Concessions Mutually Acceptable, but for the purpose of gaining time, intriguing politically and renewing their Military resources.—

In that case we should be dupes, we should give false hopes of a supply of cotton, and destroy the stimulus which although painful for the Moment is likely to be so beneficial for the future, by giving us supplies from our own possession and other parts of the world.— The probability is, that our offers would be refused by one or both belligerents, as such offers generally are, when made before they are wanted.— If the South refuse, which in consistency with their public declarations repudiating all Foreign interference they ought to do, it would hardly be a reason for recognising them.— If the North alone refused, the Question would then naturally arise, whether we ought not to recognise the South— Such a recognition, as has been explained several times to Parliament by the Government would not by itself relieve the Blockade or supply us with Cotton.— It would give no physical strength to the South, but it would greatly stimulate the North and undoubtedly assist their Government in raising Men and Money.—

By the time you receive this Letter you will probably know more of the relative position of the Combatants— At present we know that the Federals have been defeated in their attempt to Conquer the South.— But we also know that the two parties have changed parts in the great tragedy.— The Southerns instead of being invaded are become the invaders.— The chances of War are proverbially uncertain in character. . . .

It would not be a good moment to recognise the South just before a great Federal Success— If on the other hand, the Confederates continue Victorious as is to be hoped, we should stand better then than now in recognising them.—

In any case I doubt, if the War continues long after our recognition of the South, whether it will be possible for us to avoid drifting into it. . . .

I have come to the Conclusion that it is premature to depart from the Policy which has hitherto been adopted by you and Lord Palmerston, and which notwithstanding the strong Antipathy to the North, the strong sympathy with the South, and the passionate wish to have Cotton, has met with such general Approval from Parliament, the Press, and the Public.

> Yours sincerely,
> GRANVILLE.

> Woburn Abbey, October 4, 1862

My dear Palmerston,

I think unless some miracle takes place this will be the very time for offering Mediation, or as you suggest, pro-

posing to North and South to come to terms.—
   Two things however must be made clear.—
   1. That we propose separation.—
   2. That we shall take no part in the War, unless attacked ourselves.—
I will propose an Memorandum for the Cabinet on these aspects of the Question—Military—Political—and Social. . . .

Yours truly,
RUSSELL.

Woburn Abbey, October 24, 1862

My dear Palmerston.
   As no good would come of a Cabinet, I put it off.— But tho' I am quite ready to agree to your conclusions for the present, I cannot do so for G.[eorge C.] Lewis's reasons.— If there never was to be an Armistice but one which would act quite equally on both sides, and if there never was to be a peace because those who want to have it must have considered the matter, beforehand, there never would be either armistice or peace.—
   It is only by a computation of the costs and chances of going on with a war that people arrive at the conclusion they ought for their own interests to make peace.— Such a Computation many Americans have made, but they don't say it, for fear of Fort Lafayette [a famous Northern political prison].
   G. Lewis . . . says I propose that England and France and perhaps some other [?] Continental Power should ask America to suspend the War— I never thought of making such a proposal.—
   I think if Russia agreed Prussia would.— Less than the whole five would not do.— I thought it right towards the Cabinet to reserve any specific proposition. . . .

Yours truly,
RUSSELL.

— Document No. 16 —

THE GOVERNMENT MANAGES BLOCKADE RUNNING, FEBRUARY 6, 1864 [16]

By early 1864 the Confederate Government recognized that private firms engaged in blockade running were taking advantage of every opportunity to bring into the South luxury items instead of military supplies. Commodities and luxuries, of course, earned fabulous profits. In an effort to prevent waste of space on blockade runners, the Confederate Congress prohibited the importation of a long list of luxuries and also set up restrictions on exports and foreign commerce in general. Both of these "blockade statutes" were passed on February 6. The one printed below virtually nationalizes the blockade running business.

✓   ✓   ✓

A BILL TO IMPOSE REGULATIONS UPON THE FOREIGN COMMERCE OF THE CONFEDERATE STATES TO PROVIDE FOR THE PUBLIC DEFENCE

WHEREAS, the Confederate States are engaged in a war, upon the successful issue of which depend the integrity of their social system, the form of their civilization, the security of life and property within their limits as well as their existence as sovereign and independent States: *And whereas,* the condition of the contest demands that they should call into requisition whatever resources of men and money they have, for the support of their cause, and to faithfully administer the same: Therefore as a part of the system of the public defence—

[16] James M. Matthews, ed., *Statutes at Large of the Confederate States of America* (Richmond, 1864), I Congress, 4 Session, chapter XXIV.

The Congress of the Confederate States of America do enact, That the exportation of cotton, tobacco, military and naval stores, sugar, molasses and rice from the Confederate States, and from all places in the occupation of their troops, is prohibited, except under such uniform regulations as shall be made by the President of the Confederate States.

SEC. 2. That if any persons shall put, place or load, on board any ship, steamboat, or vessel, or any other water craft, or into any wagon, cart, carriage, or other vehicle for conveyance or transportation beyond the Confederate States, or into any portion of the said States occupied by the enemy, any of the articles mentioned in the first section of this act, or shall collect the same for the purpose of being conveyed or transported, contrary to the prohibition aforesaid, within the Confederate States or beyond them, the said articles, and the ship, boat, or other water craft, wagon, cart, carriage, or other vehicle, with the slaves and animals that may be employed or collected for the purpose of aiding therein, shall be forfeited, and all persons, their aiders and abettors, on conviction of being interested or concerned in the enterprise, shall be deemed to be guilty of a high misdemeanor, and punishable by such fine or imprisonment, or both, as the court may impose.

SEC. 3. That it shall not be lawful to put on board any ship, boat, vessel or other water craft, or upon any wagon, cart, carriage, or other vehicle for transportation or conveyance as aforesaid, any of the articles aforesaid, unless a permit be previously obtained from some officer of the Confederate States, specially authorized to grant the same, particularly describing the articles thus to be laden, and the ship, boat, vessel, water craft, wagon, carriage, cart, or other vehicle, on which the same is to be transported, and until bond shall be given that the same shall be conveyed and transported to the place of destination, under such conditions and regulations, and for such objects as shall be prescribed by the President under the first section of this act.

SEC. 4. That the collectors of all the districts of the Confederate States, and such other officers as may be designated by the President of the Confederate States, shall have power and authority to take into their custody any of the articles before mentioned, found on any ship, boat, or other water craft, when there is reason to believe that they are intended for exportation, or when in vessels, carts, or wagons or any other carriage or vehicle whatsoever, or, in any manner, apparently on their way towards the territories of a foreign nation, or towards the territory of the Confederate States in the occupancy of the United States, or the vicinity thereof, or towards a place whence such articles are intended to be exported, and not to permit the same to be removed until bond shall be given, with satisfactory sureties, that no violation of this act, and the regulations under the same, is intended.

Sec. 5. That the powers granted by this act to the revenue or other officers of the Confederate States under this act to allow or refuse exportation of the articles before mentioned, or for the seizure or detention of any of the said articles, shall be exercised in conformity with such instructions as the President may give through the Departments of War and of the Treasury, which instructions may impose conditions to [on] the destination and sale of the same, and the investment of the proceeds of the same, or a portion thereof, in military or other supplies for the public service, which instructions such officers shall be bound to obey; and if any action or suit shall be brought against any such officer or officers, or their agents, he or they may plead the general issue, and upon proof of a compliance with the provisions of this act, or of the regulations and instructions of the President, he or they shall be absolved from all responsibility therefor; and any person aggrieved by any of the acts of any of the officers or agents aforesaid, may file his petition before the district court of the district in which such officer or agent resides, and after due notice to him, and to the district attorney, the said court may proceed summarily to hear and determine thereupon as law and justice may require, and the judgment of the said court, and the reasons therefor, shall be filed among the records of the court. And in case any release shall be granted, the judge may impose such conditions as to giving bond and security as may, in his opinion, be necessary to secure this act from violation, and in case of refusal, may impose double or treble costs upon the petitioner, if the circumstances warrant it: *Provided,* That nothing in this act shall be construed to prohibit the Confederate States, or any of them, from exporting any of the articles herein enumerated, on their own account.

Sec. 6. That exclusive jurisdiction is conferred upon the district courts of the Confederate States, of all suits or actions that may arise under this act in behalf of the Confederate States, its officers and agents, for the recovery of all fines, penalties and forfeitures, imposed in the same, by indictment, information or action, according to the practice of the court, and the distribution of the penalties and fines shall be made, under and according to the laws now in force for violation of the revenue acts; and all laws for the mitigation and remittance of penalties and forfeitures, shall be applied in similar cases.

Sec. 7. That it shall be lawful for the President, or such officers as he may designate, to employ any portion of the military or naval forces of the Confederacy, or of the militia, to prevent the illegal departure of any ship, vessel or other water craft, or for detaining, taking possession of, and keeping in custody the same, or any wagon, cart, or other vehicle hereinbefore mentioned, their teams and drivers, and their products aforesaid, and to suppress and disperse any assembly of persons who may resist the execution of this act, or oppose the fulfillment, by the officers, of the duties imposed by the same.

Sec. 8. That this act shall expire on the day of the ratification of a treaty of peace with the United States.

Approved February 6, 1864.

— Document No. 17

A VIEW OF STONEWALL JACKSON, 1862[17]

Stonewall Jackson became more than a Confederate— he was a world hero. Apparently a religious fanatic and a dour Roundhead, he did deeds to mark him one of history's Great Captains. Natural reticence and shyness made him inarticulate about himself and so his historical image suffered considerable misconstruction. There was far more warmth and humanness about him than General Richard Taylor's interesting sketch indicates. It is given because it helped create a false Jackson for posterity.

On the second day in this camp General Winder came to me and said that he had asked leave to go to Richmond, been refused, and resigned. He commanded Jackson's old brigade, and was aggrieved by some unjust interference. Holding Winder in high esteem, I hoped to save him to the army, and went to Jackson, to whose magnanimity I appealed, and to arouse this dwelt on the rich harvest of glory he had reaped in his brilliant campaign. Observing him closely, I caught a glimpse of the man's inner nature. It was but a glimpse. The curtain closed, and he was absorbed in prayer. Yet in that moment I saw an ambition boundless as Cromwell's, and as merciless. . . .

No reply was made to my effort for Winder, and I rose to take my leave, when Jackson said he would ride with me. We passed silently along the way to my camp, where he left me. That night a few lines came from Winder, to inform me that Jackson had called on him, and his resignation was withdrawn. . . .

[17] Richard Taylor, *Destruction and Reconstruction* (New York, 1879), pp. 78-80.

I have written that he was ambitious; and his ambition was vast, all-absorbing. Like the unhappy wretch from whose shoulders sprang the foul serpent, he loathed it, perhaps feared it; but he could not escape it—it was himself—nor rend it—it was his own flesh. He fought it with prayer, constant and earnest—Apollyon and Christian in ceaseless combat. What limit to set to his ability I know not, for he was ever superior to occasion. Under ordinary circumstances it was difficult to estimate him because of his peculiarities—peculiarities that would have made a lesser man absurd, but that served to enhance his martial fame, as those of Samuel Johnson did his literary eminence. He once observed, in reply to an allusion to his severe marching, that it was better to lose one man in marching than five in fighting; and acting on this, he invariably surprised the enemy—Milroy [and] McDowell, Banks and Fremont in the Valley, McClellan's right at Cold Harbor, Pope at second Manassas.

Fortunate in his death, he fell at the summit of glory, before the sun of the Confederacy had set, ere defeat, and suffering, and selfishness could turn their fangs upon him. As one man, the South wept for him; foreign nations shared the grief; even Federals praised him. With Wolfe and Nelson and Havelock, he took his place in the hearts of English-speaking peoples.

In the first years of this century, a great battle was fought on the plains of the Danube. A determined charge on the Austrian center gained the victory for France. The courage and example of a private soldier, who there fell, contributed much to the success of the charge. Ever after, at the parades of his battalion, the name of Latour d'Auvergne was first called, when the oldest sergeant stepped to the front and answered, 'Died on the field of honor.' In Valhalla, beyond the grave, where spirits of warriors assemble, when on the roll of heroes the name of Jackson is reached, it will be for the majestic shade of Lee to pronounce the highest eulogy known to our race—'Died on the field of duty.'

— Document No. 18 —

AN INDIAN ALLIANCE, DECEMBER 21, 1861 [18]

In an attempt to win the assistance of western Indians and consequently protect the western flank of the Confederacy, the government concluded treaties with the Five Civilized Tribes and other nations in Indian territory. The Confederate commissioner, Albert Pike, proved tremendously effective and gained the friendship of most of the tribes. The treaty which follows is typical of several he negotiated.

✓   ✓   ✓

Articles of a convention entered into and concluded at the Wichita Agency, near the False Washita River, in the country leased from the Choctaws and Chickasaws, on the twelfth day of August, A. D. one thousand eight hundred and sixty-one, between the Confederate States of America, by Albert Pike, their commissioner with full powers, appointed by the President by virtue of an act of the Congress in that behalf, of the one part, and the Pen-e-tegh-ca band of the Ne-um or Comanches, and the tribes and bands of Wichitas, Cado-Ha-da-chos, Hue-cos, Ta-hua-ca-ros, A-na-dagh-cos, Ton-ca-wes, Ai-o-nais, Ki-chais, Shawnees, and Delawares residing in the said leased country, by their respective chiefs and headmen, who have signed these articles, of the other part.

ART. I. The Pen-e-tegh-ca band of the Ne-um or Comanches, and the tribes and bands of the Wichitas, Cado-Ha-da-chos, Hue-cos, Ta-hua-ca-ros, A-na-dagh-cos, Ton-ca-wes, Ai-o-nais, Ki-chais, Shawnees, and Delawares now residing within the country north of Red River and

[18] *Official Records of the Union and Confederate Armies,* Series IV, vol. 1, pp. 542-546.

south of the Canadian, and between the ninety-eighth and one hundredth parallels of west longitude, leased for them and other tribes from the Choctaw and Chickasaw Nations, do hereby place themselves under the laws and protection of the Confederate States of America in peace and war forever.

ART. II. The Confederate States of America do hereby promise and engage themselves to be during all time the friends and protectors of the Pen-e-tegh-ca band of the Ne-um, and of the Wichitas, Cado-Ha-da-chos, Hue-cos, Ta-hua-ca-ros, A-na-dagh-cos, Ton-ca-wes, Ai-o-nais, Ki-chais, Shawnees, and Delawares residing, or that may hereafter come to reside, in the said leased country; and that they will not allow them henceforward to be in any wise troubled or molested by any power or people, State or person whatever.

ART. III. The reserves at present occupied by the said several tribes and bands may continue to be occupied by them if they are satisfied therewith; and if any of them are not, the tribe or tribes, band or bands dissatisfied may select other reserves instead of those now occupied by them, in the same leased country, with the concurrence and assent of the agent of the Confederate States for the reserve Indians, at any time within two years from the day of the signing of these articles.

ART. IV. Each reserve shall be of sufficient extent of good arable and grazing land amply to supply the needs of the tribe or band that is to occupy it; and each shall have a separate reserve, unless two or more elect to settle and reside together and hold their reserves in common. The reserves shall, as far as practicable, be defined by natural boundaries that may be described, and so far as this is not practicable, by permanent monuments and definite courses and distances; and full and authentic descriptions of the reserves shall be made out and preserved by the Confederate States.

ART. V. Each tribe or band shall have the right to possess, occupy, and use the reserve allotted to it as long as grass shall grow and water run, and the reserves shall be their own property, like their horses and cattle.

ART. VI. The members of all the said several bands and tribes of Indians shall have the right, henceforward forever, to hunt and kill game in all the unoccupied part of the said leased country without let or molestation from any quarter.

ART. VII. There shall be perpetual peace and brotherhood between the Pen-e-tegh-ca band of the Ne-um or Comanches, and the tribes and bands of the Wichitas, Cado-Ha-da-chos, Hue-cos, Ta-hua-ca-ros, A-na-dagh-cos, Ton-ca-wes, Ai-o-nais, Ki-chais, Shawnees, and Delawares, between each of them and each and all of the others; and every injury or act of hostility which either has heretofore sustained at the hands of the other shall be forgiven and forgotten.

ART. VIII. The said several tribes and bands shall henceforth be good neighbors to each other, and there shall be a free and friendly intercourse among them. And it is hereby agreed by all that the horses, cattle, and other stock and property of each tribe or band and of every person of each, is his or its own, and that no tribe or band nor any person belonging to any tribe or band shall, or will hereafter kill, take away, or injure any such property of another tribe or band or of any member of any tribe or band, or in any other way do them any harm.

ART. IX. There shall be perpetual peace and brotherhood between each and all of said tribes and bands and the Cherokee, Mus-ko-ki, Seminole, Choctaw, and Chickasaw Nations; and the chiefs and headmen of each of the said tribes and bands shall do all in their power to take and return any negroes, horses, or other property stolen from white men or from persons who belong to the Cherokee, Mus-ko-ki, Seminole, Choctaw, or Chickasaw Nation, and to catch and give up any person among them who may kill or steal or do any other very wrong thing.

ART. X. None of the laws of the Choctaws and Chickasaws shall ever be in force in the said leased country so as to affect any of the members of the said several tribes and bands, but only as to their own people who may settle therein; and they shall never interfere in any way with the reserves, improvements, or property of the reserve Indians.

ART. XI. It is distinctly understood by the said several tribes and bands that the State of Texas is one of the Confederate States, and joins this convention, and signs it when the commissioner signs it, and is bound by it; and that all hostilities and enmities between it and them are now ended and are to be forgotten and forgiven on both sides.

ART. XII. None of the braves of the said tribes and bands shall go upon the warpath against any enemy whatever, except with the consent of the agent, nor hold any councils or talks with any white men or other Indians without his knowledge and consent. And the Confederate States will not permit improper persons to live among them, but only such persons as are employed by the Confederate States and traders licensed by them, who shall sell to the Indians and buy from them at fair prices, under such regulations as the President shall make.

ART. XIII. To steal a horse or any other article of property from an Indian or a white man shall hereafter be considered disgraceful, and the chiefs will discountenance it by every means in their power. For if they should not there never could be any permanent peace.

ART. XIV. The Confederate States ask nothing of the Pen-e-tegh-cas, Wichitas, Cado-Ha-da-chos, Hue-cos, Ta-hua-ca-ros, A-na-dagh-cos, Ton-ca-wes, Ai-o-nais, Ki-chais, Shawnees, and Delawares, except that they will settle upon their reserves, become industrious, and prepare to support themselves, and live in peace and quietness; and in order to encourage and assist them in their endeavors to become able to support themselves, the Confederate States agree to continue to furnish them rations of provisions in the same manner as they are now doing, to include also, sugar and coffee, salt, soap, and vinegar, for such time as may be necessary to enable them to feed themselves. They agree to furnish each tribe or band with twenty cows and calves for every fifty persons contained in the same, and one bull for every forty cows and calves; and also to furnish to all of said tribes and bands together 250 stock hogs, all of which animals shall be distributed by the agent to such persons and families as shall, in his judgment, be most proper to receive them and most likely to take care of them. And they also agree to furnish, for the use of the said tribes and bands, such number of draft-oxen, wagons, carts, plows, shovels, hoes, pickaxes, spades, scythes, rakes, axes, and seeds as may be necessary, in addition to their present supply, to enable them to farm successfully. They also agree to furnish each tribe or band annually with such quantities as the agent shall estimate for, and the superintendent require, of all such articles as are mentioned and contained in the schedule hereunto annexed, marked A; to be issued and delivered to them by the agent.

Art. XV. The Confederate States will maintain one agency for the said tribes and bands at the present agency house or some other suitable and convenient location, at which the agent shall continually reside; and they do promise the said tribes and bands that they shall never be abandoned by the agent, and that he shall not be often nor for any long time away from his agency.

Art. XVI. The Confederate States will also employ and pay an interpreter for each language spoken among the said tribes and bands, and also one blacksmith, who shall also be a gunsmith, one striker, and one wagon-maker, for all; all of whom shall reside at the agency; and they will furnish from time to time such tools and such supplies of iron, steel, and wood as may be needed for the work of the said tribes and bands; and will also furnish all the people of said tribes and bands who may be sick with medicines and medical service at the agency, where a physician shall be employed to reside for their benefit exclusively. They will also employ for five years, and as much longer as the President shall please, a farmer for each reserve to instruct the Indians in cultivating the soil, so that they may soon be able to feed themselves; and will erect such a number of horse-mills to grind their corn as the superintendent shall consider to be necessary, in order to accommodate all. And the stock and animals to be given to the tribes and bands shall be in charge of the farmers, that they may not be foolishly killed or left to perish by neglect.

Art. XVII. The Confederate States also agree to erect such buildings for the mills, and the blacksmith shops, and houses for the farmers and interpreters, as have been erected among the other Indian tribes, and also to assist the said Indians in building houses for themselves, and in digging wells for water, and opening their lands.

Art. XVIII. The said bands and tribes agree to remain

upon their reserves, and not at any time to leave them in order to make crops elsewhere. And if they should leave them the Confederate States shall not be bound any longer to feed them or make them presents or give them any assistance.

ART. XIX. The Confederate States also agree to furnish each warrior of the said tribes and bands who has not a gun with a flintlock rifle and ammunition, which he agrees never to sell or give away; and the Confederate States will punish any trader or other white man who may purchase one from them.

ART. XX. The Confederate States invite all the other bands of the Ne-um or Comanches to abandon their wandering life and settle within the leased country aforesaid, and do promise them in that case the same protection and care as is hereby promised to said tribes and bands now residing therein; and that there shall be allotted to them reserves of good land, of sufficient extent, to be held and owned by them forever; and that all the other promises made by these articles shall be considered as made to them also, as well as to the tribes and bands now residing on reserves; and that the same presents shall be made them and assistance given them in all respects; and the same things in all respects are hereby also offered the Cai-a-was and agreed to be given them if they will settle in said country, atone for the murders and robberies they have lately committed, and show a resolution to lead an honest life; to which end the Confederate States send the Cai-a-was with this talk the wampum of peace and the bullet of war, for them to take their choice now and for all time to come.

ART. XXI. The Confederate States hereby guarantee to the members of the aforesaid tribes and bands full indemnity for any horses or any other property that may be killed or stolen from them by any citizen of the Confederate States, or by Indians of any other tribe or band: Provided, That the property, if stolen, cannot be recovered and restored, and that sufficient proof is produced to satisfy the agent that it was killed or stolen within the limits of the Confederate States.

ART. XXII. If any difficulty should hereafter arise between any of the bands or tribes in consequence of the killing of any one, of the stealing or killing of horses, cattle, or other stock, or of injury in any other way to person or property, the same shall be submitted to the agent of the Confederate States, who shall settle and decide the same equitably and justly, to which settlement all parties agree to submit, and such atonement and satisfaction shall be made as he shall direct.

ART. XXIII. In order that the friendship which now exists between the said several tribes and bands of Indians and the people of the Confederate States and of the Choctaw and Chickasaw Nations may not be interrupted by the conduct of individuals, it is hereby agreed that if any white man or any Choctaw or Chickasaw injures an Indian of any one of said tribes and bands, or if any one of them injures a white man or a Choctaw or Chickasaw, no private revenge or retaliation shall take place, nor shall the Chocktaws or Chickasaws try the person who does the wrong, and punish him, in their courts, but he shall be tried and punished by the Confederate States; and the life of every person belonging to said tribes and bands shall be of the same value as the life of a white man; and any Indian or white man who kills one of them without cause shall be hung by the neck until he is dead.

ART. XXIV. It is further hereby agreed by the Confederate States that all the Texan troops now within the limits of the said leased country shall be withdrawn across Red River, and that no Texan troops shall hereafter be stationed in forts or garrisons in the said country or be sent into the same, except in the service of the Confederate States and when on the war path against the Cai-a-was or other hostile Indians.

ART. XXV. This convention shall be obligatory on the tribes and bands whose chiefs and headmen signed the same from the day of its date, and on the Confederate States from and after its ratification by the proper authority.

In perpetual testimony whereof the said Albert Pike, as commissioner with plenary powers of the Confederate States of America to the Indian nations and tribes west of Arkansas, for and on behalf of the said Confederate States, doth now hereunto set his hand and affix the seal of his arms; and the undersigned chiefs and headmen, for and on behalf of their respective tribes and bands, do now hereunto respectively set their hands and affix their seals.

Done at the Wichita Agency aforesaid on this the twelfth day of August, A. D. one thosuand eight hundred and sixty-one.

[SEAL]   ALBERT PIKE,
                              Commissioner of the Confederate States
          to the Indian Nations and Tribes West of Arkansas.

Ke-ka-re-wa, principal chief of the Pen-e-tegh-ca band of the Ne-um; To-sa-wi, second chief of the Pen-e-tegh-ca band of the Ne-um; Ca-ca-dia, second chief of the Hue-cos; Te-ats, sub-chief of the Hue-cos; O-chi-ras, principal chief of the Ta-hua-ca-ros; Pa-in-hot-sa-ma, war chief of the Pen-e-tegh-ca band of the Ne-um; I-sa-do-wa, principal chief of the Wichi-tas; A-wa-he, second chief of the Wichitas; A-sa-ca-ra, chief of the Wichitas; Ta-nah, principal chief of the Cado-Ha-da-chos; Tai-o-tun, second chief of the Cado-Ha-da-chos; Cha-wihi-win, captain of the Cado-Ha-da-chos; Cha-wah-un, captain of the Cado-Ha-da-chos; A-he-dat, principal chief of the Hue-cos; Sam Houston, second chief of the Ta-hua-ca-ros; Ca-shao, principal chief of the Ai-o-nais; Jose Maria, principal chief of the A-na-dagh-cos; Co-se-mu-so, second chief of the A-na-dagh-cos; Ke-se-mira, captain of the A-na-dagh-cos; Jim Ton-ca-we, captain of the Ton-ca-wes; Ki-is-qua, second chief of the Ki-chais; John Linny, chief of the Shawnees; Keh-ka-tus-tun, chief of the Delawares.

Signed, sealed and copies exchanged in presence of us.

Wm. Quesenbury, secretary to the commissioner; E. Rector, Superintendent of Indian Affairs for the Con-federate States; M. Leeper, agent of the Confederate States for the Wichitas and other bands; Motey Kin-naird, principal chief of the Mus-ko-kis; John Jumper, principal chief of the Seminoles; Chilly McIntosh, Isreal G. Vore, W. Warren Johnson, W. L. Pike, H. P. Jones, Charles B. Johnson, J. J. Sturm, Wm. Shirley, W. H. Faulkner.

(To the Indian names are subjoined marks.)

[Ratified December 21, 1861]

— Document No. 19 —

CONFEDERATE WAR AIMS, SEPTEMBER 7, 1862 [19]

The letter of President Davis to three of his generals given below is one of the most interesting Executive Documents. It indicates clearly a developing idea of politico-military policy on Davis' part, and shows that he had considerable knowledge of statecraft. At the same time it gives an insight into a poor military command arrangement, since it considers both General Braxton Bragg and General Edmund Kirby Smith as commanders of separate armies when, in fact, Smith should have been regarded as subordinate to Bragg.

✓　　　　✓　　　　✓

Jefferson Davis to Genl. R. E. Lee, Comdg. &c., Genl. B. Bragg, Comdg. &c., Genl. E. K. Smith, Comdg. &c.

(Probable date is Sept. 7, 1862)

Sirs:

It is deemed proper that you should in accordance with established usage announce by proclamation to the people of ＿＿＿＿＿＿＿ the motives and purposes of your presence among them at the head of an invading army, and you are instructed in such proclamation to make known,

1st. That the Confederate Government is waging this war solely for self-defence, that it has no design of conquest or any other purpose than to secure peace and the abandonment by the United States of its pretensions to govern a people who have never been their subjects and who prefer self-government to a Union with them.

2nd. That this Government at the very moment of its inauguration sent commissioners to Washington to treat

[19] Dunbar Rowland, ed., *Jefferson Davis, Constitutionalist.* . . . (10 vols.; Jackson, Miss., 1923), V, 338-339.

for a peaceful adjustment of all differences, but that these commissioners were not received nor even allowed to communicate the object of their mission, and that on a subsequent occasion a communication from the President of the Confederacy to President Lincoln remained without answer, although a reply was promised by General Scott into whose hands the communication was delivered.

3RD. That among the pretexts urged for continuance of the War is the assertion that the Confederate Government desires to deprive the United States of the free navigation of the Western Rivers although the truth is that the Confederate Congress by public act, prior to the commencement of the War, enacted that "the peaceful navigation of the Missssippi River is hereby declared free to the citizens of the States upon its borders, or upon the borders of its navigable tributaries"—a declaration to which this Government has always been and is still ready to adhere.

4TH. That now at a juncture when our arms have been successful, we restrict ourselves to the same just and moderate demand, that we made at the darkest period of our reverses, the simple demand that the people of the United States should cease to war upon us and permit us to pursue our own path to happiness, while they in peace pursue theirs.

5TH. That we are debarred from the renewal of formal proposals for peace by having no reason to expect that they would be received with the respect mutually due by nations in their intercourse, whether in peace or in war.

6TH. That under these circumstances we are driven to protect our own country by transferring the seat of war to that of an enemy who pursues us with a relentless and apparently aimless hostility: That our fields have been laid waste, our people killed, many homes made desolate, and that rapine and murder have ravaged our frontiers, that the sacred right of self defence demands that if such a war is to coninue its consequences shall fall on those who persist in their refusal to make peace.

7TH. That the Confederate army therefore comes to occupy the territory of their enemies and to make it the theatre of hostilities. That with the people of _____ themselves rests the power to put an end to this invasion of their homes, for if unable to prevail on the Government of the United States to conclude a general peace, their own State Government in the exercise of its sovereignty can secure immunity from the desolating effects of warfare on the soil of the State by a separate treaty of peace which this Government will ever be ready to conclude on the most just and liberal basis.

8TH. That the responsibility thus rests on the people of _____ of continuing an unjust and aggressive warfare upon the Confederate States, a warfare which can never end in any other manner than that now proposed. With them is the option of preserving the blessings of peace, by the simple abandonment of the design of subjugating a people over whom no right of dominion has been ever conferred either by God or man.

(Signed) Jeffn. Davis

— Document No. 20 —

LEE'S LAST REPORT TO THE PRESIDENT, APRIL 12, 1865 [20]

After he surrendered the Army of Northern Virginia on April 9, 1865, Lee faced the sad duty of reporting to President Davis the results of the Appomattox campaign. His final field report is typical of his battle accounts and contains the full and frank information which he always gave the President. In addition to a summary of the last days of the army, he added as an addenda a copy of his farewell order to his troops. General Order Number 9 stands as one of the moving documents of the Civil War. Not dramatic and not sentimental, it is nonetheless a powerful statement of affectionate appreciation.

[20] *Official Records of the Union and Confederate Armies,* Series I, vol. 46, pt. 1, pp. 1265-1267.

NEAR APPOMATTOX COURT-HOUSE, VA.,
April 12, 1865.

MR. PRESIDENT: It is with pain that I announce to Your Excellency the surrender of the Army of Northern Virginia. The operations which preceded this result will be reported in full. I will therefore only now state that, upon arriving at Amelia Court-House on the morning of the 4th with the advance of the army, on the retreat from the lines in front of Richmond and Petersburg, and not finding the supplies ordered to be placed there, nearly twenty-four hours were lost in endeavoring to collect in the country subsistence for men and horses. This delay was fatal, and could not be retrieved. The troops, wearied by continual fighting and marching for several days and nights, obtained neither rest nor refreshment; and on moving, on the 5th, on the Richmond and Danville Railroad, I found at Jetersville the enemy's cavalry, and learned the approach of his infantry and the general advance of his army toward Burkeville. This deprived us of the use of the railroad, and rendered it impracticable to procure from Danville the supplies ordered to meet us at points of our march. Nothing could be obtained from the adjacent country. Our route to the Roanoke was therefore changed, and the march directed upon Farmville, where supplies were ordered from Lynchburg. The change of route threw the troops over the roads pursued by the artillery and wagon trains west of the railroad, which impeded our advance and embarrassed our movements. On the morning of the 6th General Longstreet's corps reached Rice's Station, on the Lynchburg railroad. It was followed by the commands of Generals R. H. Anderson, Ewell, and Gordon, with orders to close upon it as fast as the progress of the trains would permit or as they could be directed on roads farther west. General Anderson, commanding Pickett's and B. R. Johnson's divisions, became disconnected with Mahone's division, forming the rear of Longstreet. The enemy's cavalry penetrated the line of march through the interval thus left and attacked the wagon train moving toward Farmville. This caused serious delay in the march of the center and rear of the column, and enabled the enemy to mass upon their flank. After successive attacks Anderson's and Ewell's corps were captured or driven from their position. The latter general, with both of his division commanders, Kershaw and Custis Lee, and his brigadiers, were taken prisoners. Gordon, who all the morning, aided by General W. H. F. Lee's cavalry, had checked the advance of the enemy on the road from Amelia Springs and protected the trains, became exposed to his combined assaults, which he bravely resisted and twice repulsed; but the cavalry having been withdrawn to another part of the line of march, and the enemy massing heavily on his front and both flanks, renewed the attack about 6 p. m., and drove him from the field in much confusion.

The army continued its march during the night, and every effort was made to reorganize the divisions which had been shattered by the day's operations; but the men being depressed by fatigue and hunger, many threw away their arms, while others followed the wagon trains and embarrassed their progress. On the morning of the 7th rations were issued to the troops as they passed Farmville, but the safety of the trains requiring their removal upon the approach of the enemy all could not be supplied. The army, reduced to two corps, under Longstreet and Gordon, moved steadily on the road to Appomattox Court-House; thence its march was ordered by Campbell Court-House, through Pittsylvania, toward Danville. The roads were wretched and the progress slow. By great efforts the head of the column reached Appomattox Court-House on the evening of the 8th, and the troops were halted for rest. The march was ordered to be resumed at 1 a. m. on the 9th. Fitz Lee, with the cavalry, supported by Gordon, was ordered to drive the enemy from his front, wheel to the left, and cover the passage of the trains; while Longstreet, who from Rice's Station had formed the rear guard, should close up and hold the position. Two battalions of artillery and the ammunition wagons were directed to accompany the army, the rest of the artillery and wagons to move toward Lynchburg. In the early part of the night the enemy attacked Walker's artillery train near Appomattox Station, on the Lynchburg railroad, and were repelled. Shortly afterward their cavalry dashed toward the Court-House, till halted by our line. During the night there were indications of a large force massing on our left and front. Fitz Lee was directed to ascertain its strength, and to suspend his advance till daylight if necessary. About 5 a. m. on the 9th, with Gordon on his left, he moved forward and opened the way. A heavy force of the enemy was discovered opposite Gordon's right, which, moving in the direction of Appomattox Court-House, drove back the left of the cavalry and threatened to cut off Gordon from Longstreet, his cavalry at the same time threatening to envelop his left flank. Gordon withdrew across the Appomattox River, and the cavalry advanced on the Lynchburg road and became separated from the army.

Learning the condition of affairs on the lines, where I had gone under the expectation of meeting General Grant to learn definitely the terms he proposed in a communication received from him on the 8th, in the event of the surrender of the army, I requested a suspension of hostilities until these terms could be arranged. In the interview which occurred with General Grant in compliance with my request, terms having been agreed on, I surrendered that portion of the Army of Northern Virginia which was on the field, with its arms, artillery, and wagon trains, the officers and men to be paroled, retaining their sidearms and private effects. I deemed this course the best under all the circumstances by which we were surrounded. On the morning of the 9th, according to the reports of the ordnance officers, there were 7,892 organized infantry with arms, with an average of seventy-five rounds of ammunition per man. The artillery, though reduced to sixty-three pieces, with ninety-three rounds of ammunition, was sufficient. These comprised all the supplies of ordnance that could be relied on in the State of Virgina. I have no accurate report of the cavalry, but believe it did not exceed 2,100 effective men. The enemy were more than five times our numbers. If we could have forced our way one day longer it would have been at a great sacrifice of life, and at its end I did not see how a surrender could have been avoided. We had no subsistence for man or horse, and it could not be gathered in the country. The supplies ordered to Pamplin's Station from Lynchburg could not reach us, and the men, deprived of food and sleep for many days, were worn out and exhausted.

With great respect, your obedient servant,

R. E. LEE,
General.

His Excellency JEFFERSON DAVIS.

ADDENDA

HDQRS. ARMY OF NORTHERN VIRGINIA

GENERAL ORDERS
No. 9   April 10, 1865

After four years of arduous service, marked by unsurpassed courage and fortitude, the Army of Northern Virginia has been compelled to yield to overwhelming numbers and resources. I need not tell the brave survivors of so many hard-fought battles, who have remained steadfast to the last, that I have consented to the result from no distrust of them. But, feeling that valor and devotion could accomplish nothing that could compensate for the loss that must have attended the continuance of the contest, I determined to avoid the useless sacrifice of those whose past services have endeared them to their countrymen.

By the terms of the agreement officers and men can return to their homes and remain until exchanged. You will take with you the satisfaction that proceeds from the consciousness of duty faithfully performed; and I earnestly pray that a merciful God will extend to you his blessing and protection.

With an unceasing admiration of your constancy and devotion to your country, and a grateful remembrance of your kind and generous considerations for myself, I bid you all an affectionate farewell.

R. E. LEE,
General.

— Document No. 21 —

JEFFERSON DAVIS' LAST MESSAGE, APRIL 4, 1865 [21]

When Lee's line was broken at Petersburg, Davis and a small official party traveled south to Danville, Virginia. Here Davis waited for word from Lee and established a temporary Confederate capital. While he knew the situation to be grave, he cherished a desperate hope that Lee and Joe Johnston might somehow link forces in North Carolina and perhaps together defeat Sherman and carry on the war in the Deep South. With his tragic false optimism came a type of eloquence which he put into a final exhortation to the Confederate people.

✓   ✓   ✓

Danville, Va. April 4, 1865.
To the People of the Confederate States of America.

The General in Chief of our Army has found it necessary to make such movements of the troops as to uncover the capital and thus involve the withdrawal of the Government from the city of Richmond.

It would be unwise, even were it possible, to conceal the great moral as well as material injury to our cause that must result from the occupation of Richmond by the enemy. It is equally unwise and unworthy of us, as patriots engaged in a most sacred cause, to allow our energies to falter, our spirits to grow faint, or our efforts to become relaxed under reverses, however calamitous. While it has been to us a source of national pride that for four years of unequaled warfare we have been able, in close proximity to the center of the enemy's power, to maintain the seat of our chosen Government free from the pollution of his presence; while the memories of the heroic dead who

[21] Dunbar Rowland, ed., *Jefferson Davis, Constitutionalist.* . . . (10 vols.; Jackson, Miss., 1923), VI, 529-531.

have freely given their lives to its defense must ever remain enshrined in our hearts; while the preservation of the capital, which is usually regarded as the evidence to mankind of separate national existence, was an object very dear to us, it is also true, and should not be forgotten, that the loss which we have suffered is not without compensation. For many months the largest and finest army of the Confederacy, under the command of a leader whose presence inspires equal confidence in the troops and the people, has been greatly trammeled by the necessity of keeping constant watch over the approaches to the capital, and has thus been forced to forego more than one opportunity for promising enterprise. The hopes and confidence of the enemy have been constantly excited by the belief that their possession of Richmond would be the signal for our submission to their rule, and relieve them from the burden of war, as their failing resources admonish them it must be abandoned if not speedily brought to a successful close. It is for us, my countrymen, to show by our bearing under reverses how wretched has been the self-deception of those who have believed us less able to endure misfortune with fortitude than to encounter danger with courage. We have now entered upon a new phase of a struggle the memory of which is to endure for all ages and to shed an increasing luster upon our country.

Relieved from the necessity of guarding cities and particular points, important but not vital to our defense, with an army free to move from point to point and strike in detail the detachments and garrisons of the enemy, operating on the interior of our own country, where supplies are more accessible, and where the foe will be far removed from his own base and cut off from all succor in case of reverse, nothing is now needed to render our triumph certain but the exhibition of our own unquenchable resolve. Let us but will it, and we are free; and who, in the light of the past, dare doubt your purpose in the future?

Animated by the confidence in your spirit and fortitude, which never yet has failed me, I announce to you, fellow-countrymen, that it is my purpose to maintain your cause with my whole heart and soul; that I will never consent to abandon to the enemy one foot of the soil of any one of the States of the Confederacy; that Virginia, noble State, whose ancient renown has [been] eclipsed by her still more glorious recent history; whose bosom has been bared to receive the main shock of this war; whose sons and daughters have exhibited heroism so sublime as to render her illustrious in all time to come; that Virginia, with the help of the people, and by the blessing of Providence, shall be held and defended, and no peace ever be made with the infamous invaders of her homes by the sacrifice of any of her rights or territory.

If by stress of numbers, we should ever be compelled to a temporary withdrawal from her limits, or those of any other border State, again and again will we return, until the baffled and exhausted enemy shall abandon in despair his endless and impossible task of making slaves of a people resolved to be free.

Let us not then despond, my countrymen, but, relying on the never failing mercies and protecting care of our God, let us meet the foe with fresh defiance, with unconquered and unconquerable hearts.

JEFFERSON DAVIS

SURRENDER TERMS AT APPOMATTOX [22]

During the retreat from Richmond and Petersburg, General Lee became increasingly aware of the desperate condition of his army. He entered into correspondence with General Grant regarding surrender terms for the Army of Northern Virginia, and when the two generals met at Appomattox, Grant wrote out his demands. Lee thought them generous and accepted. The last paragraph of the following document set the tone for much of reconstruction, since it forbade interference with paroled prisoners of war

↑ ↑ ↑

Appomattox Court House, April 9, 1865.

General R. E. Lee, commanding Confederate States Army:

In accordance with the substance of my letter to you of the 8th inst., I propose to receive the surrender of the Army of Northern Virginia on the following terms, to wit:

Rolls of all the officers and men to be made in duplicate, one copy to be given to an officer designated by me, the other to be retained by such officers as you may designate.

The officers to give their individual parole not to take arms against the Government of the United States until properly exchanged, and each company or regimental commander to sign a like parole for the men of their commands.

The arms, artillery, and public property to be parked and stacked and turned over to the officers appointed by me to receive them.

This will not embrace the side-arms of the officers, nor their private horses or baggage.

This done, each officer and man will be allowed to
return to their homes, not to be disturbed by the United
States authority so long as they observe their parole and
the laws in force where they may reside.

                              Very respectfully,
                                   U. S. Grant,
                                        Lieutenant-General.

[22] Jefferson Davis, *Rise and Fall of the Confederate Government* (2 vols.; New York, 1881), II, 659.

SELECTED BIBLIOGRAPHY

I. *Memoirs and Reminiscences*

ALEXANDER, E. P., *Military Memoirs of a Confederate* (New York, 1907).

CHESDNUT, MARY BOYKIN, *A Diary from Dixie* (New York, 1905).

DAVIS, JEFFERSON, *Rise and Fall of the Confederate Government,* 2 vols. (New York, 1881).

EARLY, JUBAL A., *Autobiographical Sketch and Narrative of the War Between the States* (Philadelphia, 1912).

GORGAS, JOSIAH, *Civil War Diary* (Tuscaloosa, Ala., 1947).

HOOD, JOHN B., *Advance and Retreat* (New Orleans, 1880).

JOHNSTON, JOSEPH E., *Narrative of Military Operations Directed During the Late War Between the States* (New York, 1874).

JONES, J. B., *A Rebel War Clerk's Diary at the Confederate States Capital,* 2 vols. (Philadelphia, 1866).

KEAN, ROBERT G. H., *Inside the Confederate Government* (New York, 1957).

LONGSTREET, JAMES, *From Manassas to Appomattox* (Philadelphia, 1896).

SORREL, G. MOXLEY, *Recollections of a Confederate Staff Officer* (2nd edition, New York, 1917).

STONE, KATE, *Brokenburn* (Baton Rouge, 1955).

TAYLOR, RICHARD, *Destruction and Reconstruction* (New York, 1879).

WRIGHT, MRS. D. GIRAUD, *A Southern Girl in '61* (New York, 1905).

II. *Government Documents and Other Primary Sources*

Journal of the Congress of the Confederate States of America, 1861-1865, 7 vols. (Washington, 1904-1905).

RICHARDSON, JAMES D., *Messages and Papers of the Confederacy,* 2 vols. (Nashville, 1906).

ROWLAND, DUNBAR, ed., *Jefferson Davis, Constitutionalist: His Letters, Papers and Speeches,* 10 vols. (Jackson, Miss., 1923).

War of the Rebellion: A Compilation of the Official Records of the Union and Confederate Armies, 127 vols. and index (Washington, 1880-1901).

III. *General Histories*

COULTER, E. MERTON, *The Confederate States of America, 1861-1865* (Baton Rouge, 1950).

EATON, CLEMENT, *A History of the Southern Confederacy* (New York, 1954).

HENRY, ROBERT S., *The Story of the Confederacy* (Indianapolis, 1931).

ROLAND, CHARLES P., *The Confederacy* (Chicago, 1960).

SCHWAB, JOHN C., *The Confederate States of America, 1861-1865* (New York, 1901).

STEPHENSON, N. W., *The Day of the Confederacy* (New Haven, 1919).

IV. *Biographies*

DURKIN, JOSEPH T., *Stephen R. Mallory: Confederate Navy Chief* (Chapel Hill, 1954).

ECKENRODE, H. J., *Jefferson Davis: President of the South* (New York, 1923).

FREEMAN, DOUGLAS SOUTHALL, *Lee's Lieutenants: A Study in Command,* 3 vols. (New York, 1942-1944).

———, *R. E. Lee: A Biography,* 4 vols. (New York, 1934-1935).

GOVAN, GILBERT, and JAMES W. LIVINGOOD, *A Different Valor: The Story of General Joseph E. Johnston* (Indianapolis, 1956).

HILL, LOUISE B., *Joseph E. Brown and the Confederacy* (Chapel Hill, 1939).

MCELROY, ROBERT, *Jefferson Davis; The Unreal and the Real,* 2 vols. (New York, 1937).

MEADE, ROBERT D., *Judah P. Benjamin: Confederate Statesman* (New York, 1943).

PARKS, JOSEPH H., *General Edmund Kirby Smith* (Baton Rouge, 1954).

STRODE, HUDSON, *Jefferson Davis,* 2 vols. (New York, 1955-1959).

VANDIVER, FRANK E., *Mighty Stonewall* (New York, 1957).

———, *Ploughshares into Swords: Josiah Gorgas and Confederate Ordnance* (Austin, 1952).

WILLIAMS, T. HARRY, *P. G. T. Beauregard: Napoleon in Gray* (Baton Rouge, 1955).

V. *Other Secondary Works*

BLACK, ROBERT C., III, *The Railroads of the Confederacy* (Chapel Hill, 1952).

BRAGG, JEFFERSON DAVIS, *Louisiana in the Confederacy* (Baton Rouge, 1941).

BRYAN, T. C., *Confederate Georgia* (Athens, 1953).

COULTER, E. MERTON, *The Civil War and Readjustment in Kentucky* (Chapel Hill, 1926).

FLEMING, WALTER L., *Civil War and Reconstruction in Alabama* (Cleveland, 1911).

JONES, ARCHER, *Confederate Strategy from Shiloh to Vicksburg* (Baton Rouge, 1961).

OWSLEY, FRANK L., *King Cotton Diplomacy* (Chicago, 1931, 1959).

———, *State Rights in the Confederacy* (Chicago, 1925).

RAMSDELL, CHARLES W., *Behind the Lines in the Southern Confederacy* (Baton Rouge, 1944).

SCHARF, J. THOMAS, *History of the Confederate States Navy* (New York, 1887).

TODD, RICHARD C., *Confederate Finance* (Athens, Ga., 1954).

VANDIVER, FRANK E., *Rebel Brass: The Confederate Command System* (Baton Rouge, 1956).

WARNER, EZRA, *Generals in Gray* (Baton Rouge, 1959).

WILEY, BELL I., *The Life of Johnny Reb* (Indianapolis, 1943).

———, *The Plain People of the Confederacy* (Baton Rouge, 1944).

———, *Southern Negroes, 1861-1865* (New York, 1938).

YEARNS, WILFRED BUCK, *The Confederate Congress* (Athens, Ga., 1960).

INDEX